PUB WALKS ALONG
The Thames Path

TWENTY CIRCULAR WALKS

Leigh Hatts

COUNTRYSIDE BOOKS
NEWBURY, BERKSHIRE

COUNTRYSIDE BOOKS
3 Catherine Road
Newbury, Berkshire

ISBN 1 85306 451 3

Designed by Graham Whiteman
Cover illustration by Colin Doggett
Photographs by the author
Maps by Jack Street

Produced through MRM Associates Ltd., Reading
Typeset by Techniset Typesetters, Newton-le-Willows, Merseyside
Printed by J.W. Arrowsmith Ltd., Bristol

Contents

Area Map Showing Location of the Walks

UPPER THAMES

BABLOCK HYTHE ⑰   OXFORD ⑯
NEWBRIDGE ⑱   CLIFTON HAMPDEN
COATES ⑳   ⑮   ⑭
    DORCHESTER
Cricklade   CAVERSHAM
    LECHLADE   Abingdon   ⑪
    ⑲
WALLINGFORD   ⑬
SOUTH STOKE ⑫   Reading

MIDDLE THAMES

Marlow
ETON ⑧
Maidenhead   Slough
Henley
⑨   Windsor   SHEPPERTON ⑦
MEDMENHAM   Staines
ASTON ⑩   Sunbury
    Egham
    Chertsey   Walton

LOWER THAMES   City

Chiswick   Chelsea
    ROTHERHITHE ①
HAMMERSMITH ③
ISLEWORTH ④   BANKSIDE ②
TWICKENHAM ⑤   *LONDON*
KINGSTON ⑥
Kingston on Thames

Walk

◦§◦

Key for Maps	
• • • • The Thames Path	→ → → Direction of Pub Walk
🏁 Start of the Pub Walk	_ . _ . _ Pub Walk incorporating the Thames Path

---

PUBLISHER'S NOTE

We hope that you obtain considerable enjoyment from this book; great care has been taken in its preparation. However, changes of landlord and actual closures are sadly not uncommon. Likewise, although at the time of publication all routes followed public rights of way or permitted paths, diversion orders can be made and permissions withdrawn.

We cannot of course be held responsible for such diversion orders and any inaccuracies in the text which result from these or any other changes to the routes nor any damage which might result from walkers trespassing on private property. We are anxious though that all details covering the walks and the pubs are kept up to date and would therefore welcome information from readers which would be relevant to future editions.

INTRODUCTION

The Thames Path had been a dream for over a century before the official opening in 1996 of the 180 mile national trail from the Thames Barrier to Kemble in Gloucestershire. At the end of the 18th century it was a reality between Putney and the source in Gloucestershire when the opening of the Thames and Severn Canal ensured a well maintained towpath. However, the 19th century saw the invention of the railways which soon led to goods increasingly being sent on the faster Great Western Railway. As the path fell into disrepair there were occasional calls for the towpath to be saved as a recreational route. In 1929 the Council for the Protection of Rural England took up the cause and exactly 40 years before the official opening of the Thames Path there was hope that Thames Conservancy's River Thames Walk Committee would have its proposals officially adopted by the post-war government. In 1977 the Ramblers' Association began its campaign and three years later Thames Water, the Conservancy's successor, gave its support. The Countryside Commission's recommendations for a route based on the towpath won government approval nine years later.

The Thames valley offers huge contrast from the tidal Thames in London's now modern Docklands to the often dry field in Gloucestershire which is the official source. In between, the long green corridor has numerous waterside villages, tranquil stretches which are never crowded, water meadows and pasture where cattle are watered by the clean river.

Greater London has a dual route with the Thames Path on both sides of the river. This arrangement ends at Kingston-upon-Thames although several rural stretches could benefit from the same generous treatment. Two are highlighted in this book. The Medmenham bank, upstream of Temple Lock and bridge in Buckinghamshire, has been included not only to embrace the historic Dog & Badger but also to enable walkers to enjoy the original towpath with the good views denied to those on the 'new' path opposite. Just upstream of Goring, the Thames Path could easily have taken the bank which has long been part of the Ridgeway national trail. Indeed thanks to the new Wallingford bypass, which has pedestrian access, it is now a serious alternative for long-distance walkers. This book opts for the alternative side so as to include the old towpath opposite Moulsford where, due to loss of ferries, the Thames Path has been banished to a main road behind the village.

The last decade has seen the closure of many pubs in town and country due to both the recession and numerous brewery amalgamations. But along the Thames pubs seem to thrive and increase. Four featured in this book can be classed as new and two, the Founders Arms and the Three Men in a Boat Tavern, are rebirths of ancient inns on sites once thought to have been lost for ever. Both have superb views which draw a steady stream of visitors.

Existing pubs seem to be enjoying a new life. The Perch and Pike is a prime example of a pub which, as recently as the Eighties, seemed slightly unwelcoming. Now it is outstanding, with a mixture of traditional sandwiches and ploughman's and very upmarket food beautifully served.

Thames pubs continue the historic role of the inn which is to provide sustenance for slow moving, long-distance travellers. The barges and stagecoaches have gone to be replaced by Thames Path walkers and river Thames holiday sailors. Both find that by nightfall they have completed around the same mileage.

These riverside pubs are increasingly offering not only real ale but local real ale from old Thames-side breweries like Fuller's of Chiswick, Brakspear's of Henley-on-Thames, Morland of Abingdon and Morrells of Oxford. The food is as good now as at any time this century and there is a noticeable increase in vegetarian dishes on the menus. Sometimes the food seems to be a greater attraction than the real ale. Thames pubs are taking advantage of the easier licensing laws to open longer on Saturdays and on summer Sundays.

The choice of pubs ranges from the large modern Docklands establishment to the remote and tiny rural inn. The ancient pubs tend to be sited close to the river crossing which they once controlled such as the Trout at St John's Bridge. In the case of the Ferryman at Bablock Hythe it is still the landlord who runs the ferry.

If you are leaving your car in a pub car park while you walk it is advisable to check with the landlord before setting out – normally there will not be any problems. Some of the London pubs lack parking space – and indeed, for example, the absence of cars on the Hammersmith riverfront is one of the features that makes the Dove so attractive.

Each pub walk is circular and is illustrated by a sketch map, designed to guide you to the starting point and give a simple but accurate idea of the route to be taken. Details of the relevant Ordnance Survey Landranger (1:50 000) and Pathfinder (1:25 000) sheets are also given – these are very useful, especially for identifying the main features of views. In London, however, it is obviously sensible to use one of the popular street maps such as the A-Z.

The walks are suitable for the casual and weekend walker. The towpath has no steep hills and families with young children might use the routes, ranging from $1\frac{1}{2}$ miles to $5\frac{1}{2}$ miles, as an introduction to walking. The Thames Path has always been intended as a route to be enjoyed in short sections and as part of a local outing as well as a national trail. But the river experience and familiar waymarking, could tempt some to want to try the entire national trail.

Included at the end of each walk is a summary of the Thames Path to help put the short route in context. Readers can 'walk' the Thames over a long period by undertaking just the short circular sections which have the advantage of exploring the often ignored hinterland. Those who have a couple of weeks to spare for a continuous walk along the Thames Path will find the pubs to be welcoming places for refreshment and, in some cases, even accommodation.

Leigh Hatts

ROTHERHITHE
The Spice Island
❧

This new pub is on the Surrey Docks riverside and the route explores the old docks, now filled in and becoming wooded, and climbs a hill for a panoramic view. The return is along recently created paths over wharves which give less well-known views of the City of London skyline as well as Limehouse and Wapping opposite.

The Spice Island, a partly timbered building resembling a boathouse, was built in 1995 on Dinorwic Wharf immediately downstream of the Surrey Docks Entrance. Alongside is Surrey Commercial Wharf where Blunn Tiles has seen huge local demand from builders as Docklands develops into a residential area.

The pub's name recalls the spice trade here and, inside, the building is more like a warehouse with ropes, hoists and chains. The brick walls are covered in old notices and photographs of Docklands past. In one corner there is a clocking on machine and a rack of cards. The toilets are found in Bay 4 West. At the back there are balconies overlooking a terrace – both viewpoints for the river and Wapping riverfront opposite. The two north bank church steeples belong to St Paul's, Shadwell, known as the Sea Captains' Church (left), and St Mary's, Cable Street. The pub half left across the water is the much older Prospect of Whitby.

The Spice Island has an informal atmosphere with Rotherhithe residents, visitors from the YHA opposite and walkers relaxing at all times of the day. Baguettes with a wide choice of fillings are available on the ground floor along with some main dishes such as chicken Provençale, and there is always a vegetarian option. The upstairs restaurant has an extensive menu. The Spice Island, a Whitbread house, can have as many as twelve cask ales available. The pub is open all day on Monday to Saturday from 11 am to 11 pm with food served until 10 pm. The Sunday opening hours are 12 noon to 10.30 pm with food served until 9 pm. Telephone: 0171 394 7108.

- **HOW TO GET THERE:** Rotherhithe is on the A200 between London Bridge and Greenwich. Rotherhithe underground station is on the East London Line.
- **PARKING:** There is a car park at the Spice Island.
- **LENGTH OF THE WALK:** 2 miles. Maps: A-Z London; OS Pathfinder 1159 City of London and 1175 Wimbledon and Dulwich; OS Landranger 177 East London (inn GR 358804).

THE WALK

From the pub walk over to the lifting bridge at the Surrey Basin entrance which gave access to nine other major docks. The first ship entered here in 1807. Do not cross the bridge but follow the harbour entrance inland by going down the steps and walking the short distance to cross the main Salter Road. Continue ahead to go down the steps to Surrey Water. This large expanse of water was once the Surrey Docks Basin. Still keep forward with the water to the right.

At the far end walk up Dock Hill Avenue, passing through (or round) a pavilion on the way. Stave Hill can be seen ahead. Cross Timber Pond Road and keep forward to reach the steps leading up to the Stave Hill viewpoint.

Stave Hill, named after filled-in Stave Dock, was built in 1986 with earth dug from the new channel linking Surrey Water to nearby Canada Water in the south-west of Docklands. From the top there are not only spectacular views of the City skyline but also Crystal Palace and the

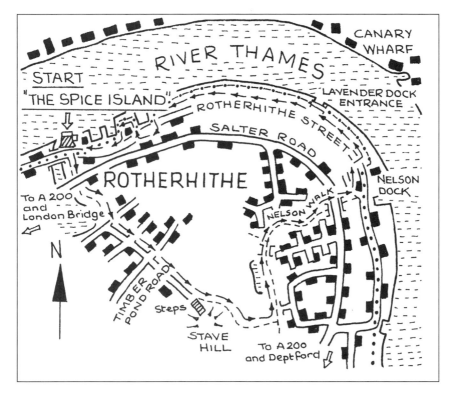

ever present Canary Wharf. The immediate view can be compared with the relief map showing the area as a network of docks, the position of Stave Hill marked by a knob. This walk will lead to Nelson Dock on the Thames, seen on the map between Acorn and Lavender Docks. Looking in that direction now you can see the masts of the ship in the dry dock. This ship was once a French Navy training vessel.

The walk continues to the left of the steps. (Turn right if descending from Stave Hill.) Just before completing the half circle go left. At a junction turn left to follow a winding path. A bridge joins from the right where there is water. Soon there is a large, deep pond to the left. Stay on the main path and after a double bend the path crosses a bridge (with a ford to the left).

Here, at a wide junction, turn right on a path known as Nelson Walk. This soon crosses the water by bridge and ford. At a junction keep forward downhill to pass under the main Salter Road. Shortly there is a view ahead of Nelson Dock House built in 1740. Go left to reach the road ahead opposite the former Mills & Knight Ltd building.

Nelson Dock, now part of a Holiday Inn, takes its name from the 17th-century owner. Between the 1750s and 1821 Randall & Brent pioneered steam shipbuilding and in the 1850s Bilbe & Perry pioneered timber cladding on iron frames for China tea clippers.

Turn left to pass the Blacksmiths Arms and Canada Wharf and turn right up an alley at the side known as Horn Stairs. Turn left onto a wide terrace giving a view across to Canary Wharf. Walk upstream past houses built in 1994-5 on Ordnance Wharf leadworks which closed in 1982. Continue along the riverside to pass a decorative obelisk and Pageants Stairs. After a short distance cross the former Lavender Dock entrance to reach Sovereign View, a housing development completed in 1993 on Lavender Wharf occupied until 1985 by Burmah Castrol's oil depot.

At Globe Stairs the path returns to the road opposite the Three Compasses. Turn right to walk round Globe Wharf Rice Mill built in 1883 to handle rice coming into London. Turn right up the far side of Globe Wharf to walk along King & Queen Wharf. Go through gates onto the higher level Prince's Riverside or, if the gates are locked, return to the road here and go right. Pass Bull Head Dock where the *Téméraire*, painted by Turner, was broken up.

Ahead is the Surrey Dock entrance bridge and the Spice Island.

THAMES PATH - ROTHERHITHE TO BANKSIDE (2³/₄ MILES)

Using the south bank route, from the Spice Island the Path stays with the river except for inland diversions in Rotherhithe village centre, at Chambers Wharf and in the Southwark Cathedral area.

WALK 2

BANKSIDE
The Founders Arms

❧

Bankside is the former garden of Winchester Palace where Bishops of Winchester lived until the 17th century and the view from this country estate was the City of London dominated by St Paul's Cathedral. The panorama from traffic free Bankside is still splendid and this walk visits the far City bank for a look back to Bankside which once again has the Globe Theatre on its riverside as well as the new Tate Gallery. Both the north bank and south bank routes of the Thames Path are included in this circuit.

The Founders Arms is a modern polygonal, glass walled structure with a superb view of St Paul's Cathedral across the river. Indeed the pub, which claims to have 'the finest view in London', is on the site of the foundry where the cathedral's bells were cast so it was the Dean of St Paul's who in 1979 was invited to perform the opening ceremony. The pub sign shows the arms of the Founders Company. The Falcon Point flats behind take their name from the Falcon Inn which was demolished in 1808.

There is a wide terrace with tables for good views. Inside you will find a long bar and comfortable chairs, and high stools facing the river with panorama photographs to help visitors identify the city buildings. The walls have plenty of old prints of the bridges.

Baguettes come filled with ham or tuna fish and salad and ploughman's feature Cheddar, Brie, Danish Blue, ham and pâté. Scampi and Cumberland sausage have salad garnish and chips or new potatoes. There is also a table service restaurant at one end. This is a Young's house with their Bitter, Special and Winter Warmer. The Founders Arms is open all day from 11 am to 11 pm (10.30 pm on Sundays) with food available until 9.30 pm. Telephone: 0171 928 1899.

- **HOW TO GET THERE:** Bankside is the Thames' south bank opposite the City of London and is best reached by walking south from Blackfriars station over Blackfriars Bridge and turning left onto the riverside path.
- **PARKING:** There is no car park at the pub and parking in nearby Hopton Street is very limited.
- **LENGTH OF THE WALK:** 1½ miles. Maps: A-Z London; OS Pathfinder 1159 City of London; OS Landranger 176 West London or 177 East London (inn GR 319806).

THE WALK

Walk downstream to pass Bankside Power Station which from the year 2000 is the Tate Gallery's Museum of Modern Art. Just beyond the huge brick building is a low terrace of houses. Cardinal Cap Alley is the last of the medieval passages leading from the river. Cardinal's Wharf with the red door was a pub where ferrymen met in 1613 to discuss their future when the first Globe burned down. On the other side of the passage is the Provost's Lodging – home of the Provost of Southwark Cathedral and the only deanery to have a view of the wrong cathedral. The Globe is a reconstruction completed in 1996 of Shakespeare's theatre which stood in nearby Park Street from 1599 until 1644 when the Roundheads shut theatres. The Bishop of Winchester, unlike the Lord Mayor of London on the north bank, was happy to rent ground to players.

Where the promenade ends continue ahead along the riverside road to pass the end of Bear Gardens. The Shakespeare Education Centre in this cobbled lane contains the successor theatre to the Hope Theatre

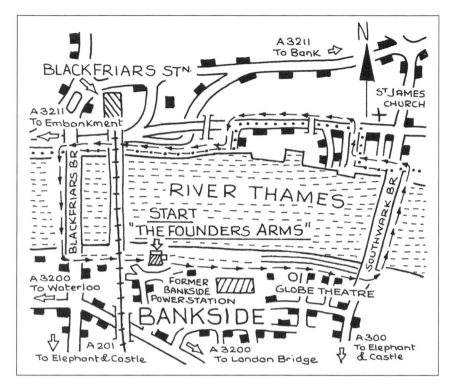

which staged both plays and bear baiting in Elizabeth I's reign. Ben Jonson's *Bartholomew Fair* was premièred here in 1614. In the wall at the river end is a ferryman's seat where some say Shakespeare sat and waited for a ferry to take him back to his home in the former Blackfriars Priory site. Ahead is Southwark Bridge, a 1920s structure, replacing the 1819 toll crossing featured in Dickens' *Little Dorrit*. Underneath is a map of Bankside as known to Dickens.

Go up the steps onto the bridge, leaving the Thames Path (south) to continue under it. On the downstream side there is the Financial Times building. Walk over the Thames towards the north bank. It was between this bridge and downstream Cannon Street railway bridge that in 1989 the *Marchioness* sank after hitting the *Bowbelle*. Ahead on the upstream side is Vintners Place built in 1992 as part of Vintners' Hall to a design inspired by St Peter's in Rome. The Prince of Wales arrived by river to open the building.

 Go down the steps on the left to walk under the Vintners Place portico and follow Kennett Wharf Lane to Upper Thames Street.

Opposite is St James Garlickhythe church with St James the Great depicted holding his pilgrim staff on top of the clock. Go left along the road to pass the turning to medieval Queenhithe. Keep by the main road to go under Queensbridge House. The way ahead is now High Timber Street with Stew Lane and Gardener's Lane off to the left. The lonely church tower on the far side of the road belonged to St Mary Somerset which was demolished in 1871.

Do not go ahead into the tunnel but left to Broken Wharf to regain the river. Here there is a direct view of the Provost's Lodging on the far bank. Follow the wide riverside path past Swiss Bank House and the new City of London School building opened in 1986. Go under Blackfriars railway bridge but at the road bridge climb the steps, leaving the Thames Path. Once on Blackfriars Bridge turn left to cross the river.

The first Blackfriars road bridge opened in 1769 here at the confluence of the Fleet and Thames on the north side – the Fleet now emerges under the present 1869 bridge near where Italian banker Robert Calvi was found hanged in 1982. The railway bridge dates from 1884. Between the two are the piers of the first railway bridge erected in 1862 to carry the main continental trains and demolished in 1985. There is a good view of the Oxo Tower built in 1930 when it was London's controversial second highest commercial building.

At the south end of the bridge is Express Newspapers' Ludgate House standing on the site of the burned out Albion flour mill which inspired the 'dark satanic mills' in William Blake's poem *Jerusalem*. Opposite is Doggett's Coat and Badge pub, named after the annual rowing race which has passed here since 1715. Go left at the Express building to go down steps onto the riverside path and turn right to pass under the railway. Keep by the river to reach the Founders Arms.

THAMES PATH - BANKSIDE TO HAMMERSMITH (10 MILES)

On the south bank route, from the Founders Arms the Thames Path stays by the river as far as Vauxhall Bridge. There are a couple of road diversions before the big but probably temporary inland route round Battersea Power Station. In contrast the next section is through Battersea Park and all along the waterfront to the Olympia line railway bridge. The route is waymarked in and out of the Wandsworth riverside to Putney where the towpath officially begins. The Dove at Hammersmith is on the north bank after Hammersmith Bridge.

WALK 3
HAMMERSMITH
The Dove

❧❀❧

The Dove is on Hammersmith's attractive riverfront and this route goes through even more charming Chiswick with its large riverside houses to St Nicholas' church in the old village centre. Use is made of the new Corney Reach path to stay by the river. Barnes railway bridge's footbridge offers a handy crossing to visit Barnes before following a surprisingly rural towpath offering the best views of Chiswick and the river. This is part of the famous University Boat Race course known to so many through television.
The walk follows the Thames Path on both sides of the river.

The Dove, often wrongly called the Doves although the name with an s was once painted on the building, is The Pigeons in A.P. Herbert's *The Water Gypsies*. By tradition the sign outside always includes the landlord's name. In the 18th century this was the Dove Coffee House with a claim that 17th-century customers included Charles II and Nell Gwynne. A later visitor was painter Turner, an admirer of James Thomson who is said to have written the words for *Rule Britannia* upstairs. Certainly his now less well-known *The Seasons* was written here when he was suffering from a fatal fever caught on a river trip. H.G. Wells, Ernest Hemingway and Graham Greene are among many patrons who are listed on the downstairs wall.

The interior is partly flagstone floor and at the back there is a popular vine-covered conservatory entrance to the river terrace. The bar has plenty of historic photographs of the Dove and Doves. This is a tiny pub which according to the *Guinness Book of Records* has the smallest public bar. Men should beware of the very narrow toilet where you can easily jam your hand in the door. (With such confined space the Dove does not welcome children so those accompanied by under-aged persons should walk upstream to the nearby Old Ship.)

At the Dove an extensive menu is available on the upper floor. Popular baguettes filled with tuna or egg and mayonnaise come with orange and carrot salad, and there are jacket potatoes, vegetable pie and plenty of specials including a good range of puddings such as summer pudding with cream. In addition, Thai food is served in the evenings. The beer is local Fuller's which has been brewed on the same riverside Chiswick site since Charles II's reign and this has been a Fuller's house since 1796. The pub is open all day on Monday to Saturday from 11 am to 11 pm with food offered from 12 noon until 3 pm and 6 pm to 10 pm on weekdays but 12 noon to 5 pm only at weekends. Sunday opening hours are 12 noon to 10.30 pm. Telephone: 0181 748 9474.

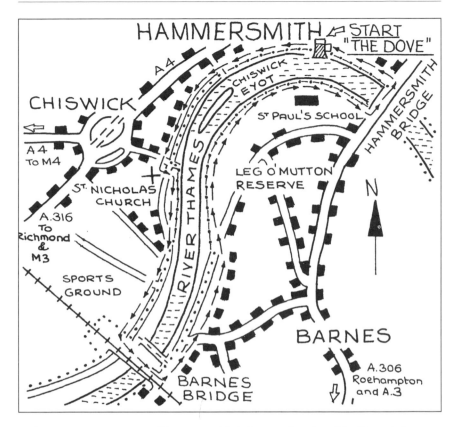

- **HOW TO GET THERE:** Hammersmith is in west London. The Dove is in an alley off riverside Furnival Gardens which is best reached by going south down Nigel Playfair Avenue, between the Virgin cinema and the Town Hall, in Hammersmith's King Street. A tunnel leads under the main Great West Road. The nearest station is Ravenscourt Park.
- **PARKING:** There is no parking at the pub and nearby street parking is extremely limited.
- **LENGTH OF THE WALK:** 4 miles. Maps: A-Z London; OS Pathfinder 1175 South London; OS Landranger 176 West London (inn GR 227784).

THE WALK

Turn left out of the pub. The lane opens just before Kelmscott House where William Morris once lived. The house takes its name from Morris's country house upstream near Lechlade. Emery Walker (see over) helped to run the Kelmscott Press from the house.

Continue along the riverside to pass Weltje Road where the corner house has a plaque recalling artist Eric Ravilius' five years here. Still keep forward when the road ends and walk under an arcade to find the Old Ship, dating from 1815. Follow the path to the Black Lion at Hammersmith Terrace where the houses still have riverside gardens. There are three blue plaques in this street – Edward Johnston who designed the London Transport typeface at number 3; typographer and printer Sir Emery Walker at number 7 and A.P. Herbert, author, humorist and MP, at number 12. Johnston thought the area had the advantages of town and country combined.

Beyond the corner shop the road rises briefly to enter Chiswick – there is a boundary stone by Cedar House on the right – where the riverside houses give way to gardens belonging to the house on the right. The island, Chiswick Eyot, is the home of Canada geese, ducks and herons. The drawdock was once used by Fuller's brewery to land hops and malt. Walpole House, named after the first prime minister, whose relatives lived here, was the home of Barbara Villiers who bore Charles II three children. Ahead is Chiswick church which has a 15th-century tower and artist William Hogarth buried in a fenced tomb by the path.

Do not go ahead but left through a small gate (open daylight hours only) on the right side of the drawdock to reach the riverside. At first the path is over Church Wharf, once occupied by Thornycroft shipbuilding which moved to Southampton in 1904 when destroyers became too large to pass under bridges, and then Corney Reach which is a housing development on the site of Corney House visited by Elizabeth I in 1602. Beyond Chiswick Pier there is a riverside lane before the path joins a cycleway to run along the edge of a riverside sports ground with a view of Barnes. Stay by the river when the metalled surface ends but go behind the boathouse as the Thames Path signs indicate.

Once in front of the railway embankment (there is a Civil Service Sports Ground sign) go left along a passage and up steps onto the footbridge attached to Barnes Bridge in the 1890s and made strong enough to withstand the Boat Race crowds.

On the far side of the river go right from the steps to walk downstream past the home of composer Gustav Holst, marked with a blue plaque. Barnes High Street is to the right but the walk continues ahead on the riverside path. Soon the river bends away leaving the towpath to run past the woodland of the Leg O'Mutton

Reserve. This is a former drinking water reservoir now home to 70 species of bird including herons. Later the rural feel is preserved by St Paul's School playing fields. There are fine views of Corney Reach, Chiswick and the Dove. On approaching Hammersmith Bridge there is the best view of Hammersmith church (by the flyover) where the bridge's designer, William Tierney Clark, is buried.

Cross the bridge and go right down the steps.

Walk upstream, once again on the Thames Path, along riverside Lower Mall. Look in the wall between numbers 6 and 7 to see a piece of stone from Henley church upstream. The Blue Anchor opened in 1720. The path runs into Furnival Gardens which only date from 1936 when a creek was filled in. Go up the alley behind the houses ahead and find the Dove.

THAMES PATH - HAMMERSMITH TO ISLEWORTH (4 MILES)

From Barnes Bridge, on this walk, the south bank route of the Thames Path faithfully follows the towpath through Mortlake and Kew as far as Richmond Lock. At weekends in the summer Isleworth, passed on the far bank, can be reached by ferry, and at other times by following the final section of Walk 4 over Richmond Lock.

WALK 4

ISLEWORTH
The London Apprentice
ঔষ্টৈৣ

Isleworth is a good example of how the river maintains a green corridor through the capital. Here there is a rural feel although suburbia is nearby. The walk passes a country mansion and explores the confluence of the rivers Brent and Thames before taking the towpath alongside Kew Gardens. This circuit is best undertaken on summer weekends when the ferry is operating. But other times are also rewarding when the first lock on the river provides the crossing back to the north bank. Both routes of the Thames Path are included, north and south of the river.

Although the earliest record of a licence here is 1731 there has been an inn on the site for around 500 years. The London Apprentice now has an 18th-century exterior and a name which recalls the apprentices who rowed up from the City of London to this village on their annual day off. Patrons have included Henry VIII and Charles II. Also alleged to have drunk here is Lady Jane Grey who visited whilst engaged in a conspiracy to take the throne from Mary I. The 20th century saw flight pioneers Sir John Alcock and Sir Arthur Brown as regular visitors during the First World War. The river location is a great attraction and until 1739 the London Apprentice was open day and night to serve travellers by water and horse. Some may have been smugglers landing their booty at nearby All Saints' church which was linked to the pub by an underground passage.

Inside there are several historic photographs showing the pub and river. The first floor restaurant, noted for its Italian ceiling dating from about 1600, is called the Eight's Room after the eight branches of vine in the ceiling decoration, Henry VIII and the rowing eights. The downstairs conservatory opening onto the terrace has buffet food such as Cheddar, Stilton, Brie or pâté ploughman's, soup, baked potato with tuna topping, ham baguettes and main dishes such as Cumberland sausage in batter with chips and peas. Puddings can include apple crumble and custard. This is an Inntrepreneur house with John Smith's Bitter, Courage Best Bitter and Wadworth 6X. The London Apprentice is open all day on Monday to Saturday from 11 am to 11 pm and on Sundays from 12 noon to 10.30 pm. Food is always available until 8 pm but on Sundays, unusually, until closing time. Telephone: 0181 560 1915.

- **HOW TO GET THERE:** Isleworth is on the river just south of Busch Corner on the A315 west of Brentford. The nearest station is Syon Lane but the H37 bus stops at Busch Corner.
- **PARKING:** There is limited parking on the wharf outside the church.
- **LENGTH OF THE WALK:** 5½ miles. Maps: A-Z London; OS Pathfinder 1174 Hounslow; OS Landranger 176 West London (inn GR 168761).

THE WALK

● Walk towards the ferry point opposite the church. The church's nave was destroyed by arson in 1943 and rebuilt to a design by Michael Blee in 1969, incorporating the 15th-century tower. Bodies of Great Plague victims were brought here by barge and buried behind the church. Follow the pavement inland round the churchyard – from the road it is possible to see the tablets recording flood levels. After a short distance go right through the Syon Park gateway to follow the estate road.

Soon there is a view to the right of Syon House, home of the Duke of Northumberland, but originally a monastery and convent. (At the

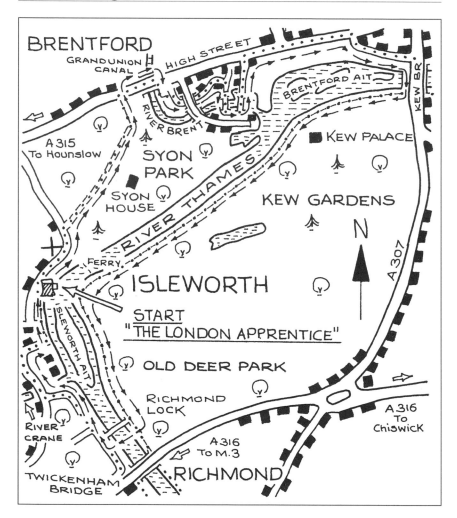

Reformation the sisters went abroad and now the community is in Devon.) Lady Jane Grey made her bid to oust Mary from here. The two lodges were added by the 9th Earl of Northumberland who spent 17 years in the Tower of London accused of involvement in the Gunpowder Plot.

Continue past the garden centre. The 14th-century monastic barn, occupied by a health food shop, is the oldest surviving building. It has a plaque to St Richard Reynolds, a monk who was executed for taking Catherine of Aragon's side against Henry VIII. The road narrows to become a walled footpath leading to the main road. It was around here that the battle of Brentford was fought in 1642 when Royalists took the town, slashing fishing nets and driving defenders into the Thames.

Turn right to cross the Grand Union Canal and go right down steps onto the towpath. After a short distance go sharp left to take the steps up and down over the wall and along a lane. Ahead is the tower of Brentford's former church which the poet Shelley attended as a schoolboy. Go right into The Ham. Beyond the former railway bridge follow the steps to rejoin the canal and take more steps up onto the footbridge. On the far side of the canal go sharp left down to the water and along the path. Beyond the lock go up the steps to cross the road bridge giving a view of the confluence of the canal – also the river Brent – with the Thames. Follow Dock Road to reach Brentford High Street. Ahead is the spire of St Paul's church.

Go right along Brentford High Street for 1/4 mile. At the T-junction with Ealing Road go right down the wide steps. Before reaching the river go left through a barrier and right to a riverside path. Steps take the path up to a higher level at Waterman's Art Centre. Continue along the high path overlooking the river. During the 17th century bricks, fruit and fish went to London by barges which returned with horse dung ballast for use as fertiliser – there was a Dung Wharf. The island, Brentford Ait, was planted with trees in the 1920s to screen Brentford's now demolished gasworks. Inland is the former St George's church which has become the Musical Museum.

It is necessary to briefly return to the road. Ahead is the 1867 tower of a pumping station (now Kew Bridge Steam Museum) which had river water pumped up it to run down into the water mains. Just beyond O'Riordans Tavern turn back to the river to continue along a riverside path known as The Hollows where there are usually several houseboats.

Cross Kew Bridge, leaving the north bank Thames Path to continue under it, and on the far side go down steps and walk back to the towpath. Do not go under the bridge but walk upstream.

Soon the high path passes Kew Palace, built in 1631 and the smallest Royal palace. George III spent his last years here when the garden was subject to flooding and Queen Victoria's parents were married in the drawing room. Later there is the Brent Ferry Gate entrance. The ferry ceased to run at the outbreak of the Second World War.

Soon there is a view across the river to Brentford's St Paul's church and the Grand Union Canal entrance – both seen earlier. This is a good stretch of towpath to see herons. Later Syon House is across on the far tide meadow, the natural creeks of which are washed twice daily by freshwater pushed back by the North Sea. The Northumberland lion crest on the roof was once on the family's town house in Trafalgar Square.

Isleworth and the London Apprentice come into view. The white residence began as a Tudor boathouse and then was converted during the Georgian period into a teahouse. On summer weekends Isleworth can be reached by a ferry which operates from May to September.

Those continuing on the full route simply follow the towpath ahead alongside the tree-lined Old Deer Park with modern Isleworth hidden by Isleworth Ait. On turning south-east there is Richmond half-tide weir and the Thames' first lock which saves Richmond from a dramatic drop in water level at low tide.

Cross the high level walkway.

On the far bank go right to walk downstream along the road. When the road swings away keep ahead on a narrow path. The way soon opens out giving a good view of houseboats. At Manresa College, part of Brunel University, go inland to follow a road to a junction. Turn right over the river Crane and follow the road as it double bends alongside the grounds of Nazareth House convent. At the far end turn right down Lion Wharf Road to rejoin the river. Go left to pass in front of the Town Wharf pub on a path which crosses two bridges – the second is over the man-made Duke of Northumberland's River – before running inland to emerge by an archway inside Bridge Wharf. Go through the arch and right along the road to reach the London Apprentice.

THAMES PATH - ISLEWORTH TO TWICKENHAM (2½ MILES)

From Richmond half-tide weir the towpath route of the Thames Path continues on the south side. Twickenham is on the north bank beyond Richmond Bridge.

TWICKENHAM
The White Swan
❧

The walk takes in two country houses linked by a reliable ferry and visits the little church where the Queen Mother's parents were married. At Richmond there is a view of the new classical riverfront development before the return route affords the best views of Richmond Hill and Petersham Meadows below.

The riverside White Swan often has white swans passing and has been justifiably described as 'everything tourists hope an English pub will be'. Here it is genuine too for it opened in 1690. But Twickenham is even better known for its rugby ground so it's appropriate that there is a rugby room at the back with rugby shirts and autographed balls. In the main room there are plenty of old pictures of the riverside including a framed article from a 1944 *Country Life* mentioning the pub. Ornaments on shelves and old papers by the fireplace give it a homely feel. Apart from rugby enthusiasts, it is also popular with many in high powered jobs who have left their business cards above the bar. A popular corner of this pub is the triclinium – three-sided room – which has window seats. The bar is on the first floor, reached by an outside staircase, and in summer many sit out on one of the delightful balconies with its attractive balustrade or take advantage of the secluded position by sitting at the tables across the road at the waterside.

Eel Pie Island opposite is named after a dish served on the island from the 16th century until earlier this century when it still had its own pub. Food at the White Swan, often prepared by a chef who worked downstream at the Savoy, includes soup, home-cooked ham and ploughman's. Sunday lunches are a speciality. This is a freehouse with Webster's Yorkshire Bitter and guest ales. It is open from 11 am to 3 pm and 5.30 pm to 11 pm but all day at weekends (including Fridays) and all week in summer. Food is available from 12 noon to 3 pm and, except Sundays, 7 pm to 9 pm. Telephone: 0181 892 2166.

- **HOW TO GET THERE:** Twickenham is just west of Richmond on the A305. The White Swan is in Riverside on the Twickenham riverfront. Twickenham station is nearby.
- **PARKING:** There is limited street parking nearby.
- **LENGTH OF THE WALK:** 3½ miles. Maps: A-Z London; OS Pathfinder 1174 Hounslow; OS Landranger 176 West London (inn GR 167734).

THE WALK

Turn left from the pub to pass Lebanon Park and the old ferry point recalled by Ferry Cottage. The walled road double bends to run under a footbridge. To the left is Orleans House Gallery – all that remains of Orleans House built in 1710 and later named after Louis Philippe, the future King of France, who spent three years in exile here. Turn right to leave the road and follow a path to the riverside. Just by a children's play area there is a direct view across the river to Old Father Thames sitting outside Ham House's front door. On leaving the gardens the way is alongside the grounds of Marble Hill House. After a few yards there is Hammerton's Ferry which runs daily. The north bank Thames Path, your return route, continues straight on. Take the boat across to the far bank – small fare payable.

The ferry lands passengers at steps. Go straight over the towpath to follow a short concrete path and turn right through a gate. The right-hand path runs to the front of Ham House, built in 1610 and little changed since the Earl of Lauderdale (the L in Charles II's Cabal) and

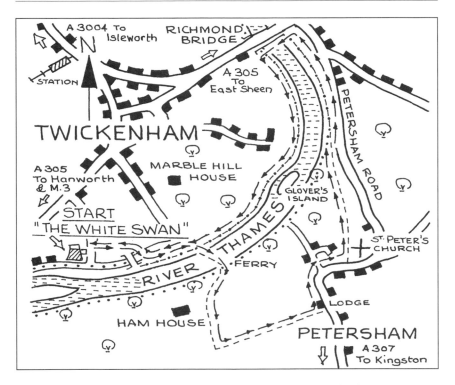

his wife made it their home. The garden, open daily free, is a rare survival of the formal 17th-century style. Ham House is in the care of the National Trust (admission charge) which encourages visitors to arrive either on foot or by boat as in the 17th century.

Go up the left side of the house where the path is divided for walkers and horseriders. There is a view of the garden on the way through the wall. At the far end (except to look at the garden through the gates to the right) go left on a long, straight metalled path. This is one of the former driveways to Ham House and ahead can be seen the archway flanked by lodges. On reaching the lodges bear round to the right to avoid the archway and reach the road at Petersham.

To the right is the Fox and Duck and ahead Farm Lodge. Turn left along the road and at the junction with River Lane bear round to the right with the main road to pass between Rutland Lodge on the left and Montrose House – both fine 17th-century houses. Continue along the road and go left where St Peter's church is signposted. A lane passes the little church which dates from the 13th century but is now noted for its box pews, galleries and two-decker pulpit. Lord Lauderdale of Ham

House married here and so also did the Queen Mother's parents in 1881. George Vancouver, who lived at Navigator's Cottage in River Lane and discovered Vancouver Island, is buried by the churchyard's south wall. Continue down the lane and at the bend keep ahead along a hedged metalled footpath. Beyond a barrier the path runs across Petersham Meadows where the grazing cows are claimed to be the nearest to central London. At a kissing-gate on the far side go ahead along the wide path.

After passing the rustic tunnel entrance to Terrace Gardens the path joins the riverside. Ahead is a fine view of Richmond Bridge. After passing Richmond landing stage, and before reaching the bridge, go to the right of the towpath wall to follow a winding path up to the bridge, leaving the Thames Path again.

Richmond Bridge dates from 1777 when it cost a halfpenny to walk over. Now it's free and there is a good view of the late 20th-century neo-classical riverside development by Quinlan Terry. On the far side go left down the steps (or ahead to the end of the fence at high tide) to walk upstream.

This 'north bank' path has signs of flood defences. There are good views of the towpath and soon Petersham Meadows and the huge Star and Garter Home on Richmond Hill. Across the far meadows can be seen the Italianate tower of All Saints which was intended in 1907 as a successor to Peterham's tiny village church.

As Glover's Island blocks the view there may be sight of a floating hermit's home which for years has evaded Port of London Authority regulations. Ahead on the path are the grounds of Marble Hill House (open to the public) completed in 1729 for George II's mistress Lady Suffolk. In 1795 Mrs Fitzherbert, the Prince Regent's first wife, lived here. The house, with an interior compared with Wilton House and Versailles, is open daily (admission charge). Look just inside the first gate to see the country's largest black walnut tree which is at least as old as the house.

Keep ahead to pass Hammerton's Ferry and follow the outward route, through the riverside gardens and along the walled road, to the White Swan.

THAMES PATH - TWICKENHAM TO KINGSTON (3¹/₂ MILES)

The Thames Path continues on both banks but the towpath is on the Ham House side and runs continuously by the river to Kingston.

WALK 6
KINGSTON-UPON-THAMES
The Bishop out of Residence
❦

Kingston means 'King's stone' and this can be seen outside the Guildhall.
King Alfred chose to be crowned on the stone in an attempt to unite with
Mercia on the north bank against the Danes who came upriver. From the

historic riverside location, a few yards from Kingston's attractive Market Place, the walk crosses the river for a stroll in Hampton Court Park where sheep and deer graze. There is the chance of a ferry ride back in season.

The Bishop out of Residence only opened in 1979 and the name, chosen in a competition, refers to a previous house on the site used by the Bishop of Winchester, William of Wykeham, in the 14th century. Bishops of Winchester held land here from 1202 and this became a resting point on the journey between Wolvesey Castle in Winchester and Winchester Palace next to London Bridge in Southwark. All three residences were in the vast Diocese of Winchester – the Southwark Diocese with its Suffragan Bishop of Kingston is a 20th-century invention. Bishop Wykeham died in 1404 and the house was rented to a brewer who entertained Henry V here in 1414. From around 1663 to 1963 the site was a tannery which gave out a slightly unpleasant smell.

This is a popular pub but there is a quieter bar upstairs and tables on an adjoining balcony. The windows look downstream to Kingston Bridge. This may be a Young's pub but most people come here for the food. The huge menu includes mackerel, ham, Cheddar or Brie ploughman's, sandwiches, jacket potatoes and several vegetarian dishes. Specials can include lamb chops or a large haddock served with chips. There are also usually four or five pudding choices. Sunday roast is popular. The weekday opening hours are 11 am to 11 pm, and the Sunday times are 12 noon to 10.30 pm. Food is served from opening time to 3.30 pm. Telephone: 0181 546 4965.

- **HOW TO GET THERE:** Kingston-upon-Thames is on the A308, between Wandsworth and Hampton Court. The riverside Bishop out of Residence is near Kingston Bridge and is reached from Thames Street by going down a road called Bishop's Hall. The nearest station is Kingston.
- **PARKING:** There is no parking at the pub or on the riverside although public car parks are nearby.
- **LENGTH OF THE WALK:** 2½ miles. Maps: A-Z London; OS Pathfinder 1190 Weybridge, Hampton Court and Esher; OS Landranger 176 West London (inn GR 179698).

THE WALK

Turn right out of the pub's riverside door and go up the bridge steps (or slope) and cross the river. Until 1738 this was the first bridge above London Bridge. Once on the Middlesex bank turn left

down Barge Walk to reach the river bank. There are usually houseboats here. Opposite is the Bishop out of Residence and the Hogsmill River, which rises near Epsom, can be seen flowing into the Thames. After ½ mile there is the 1850 Italianate tower of St Raphael's church on the far bank. Here there may be Hart's Ferry operating, offering the chance to return to the Kingston bank and walk back into the town.

The path curves south-west to pass Raven's Ait. The island, now a residential watersport centre, was largely an osier ground in the 19th century. The area on the far bank is known as Seething Wells, recalling therapeutic springs.

Where the island ends turn inland across the grass, leaving the Thames Path, and go through a small gate. (Behind there is a direct view across the river to the 1860 spire of St Mark's in Surbiton – the rest of the church was destroyed in the war.) The grass path runs straight ahead between high fences hiding paddocks. Beyond the gate at the far end, leading into Hampton Court Park, bear half right to pass The Rick Pond and join a metalled road. With the pond to the left there is on the right another pond – this is the overflow to the $3/4$ mile long Long Water ahead which reaches almost to Hampton Court Palace.

At a junction go right with the end of the Long Water to the left – go up on to the bank to see the view of the Palace. Continue along the road, leaving the water behind. This is a good area for deer. Sometimes there are also sheep. The park was enclosed by Henry VIII and it was here that prisoner Charles I made a break for freedom in 1647 by riding out of the gates for the south coast. At a junction bear right and ignore all turnings. Kingston can be seen to the right in the distance. Eventually the road runs downhill, with Hampton Wick Pond over to the left, towards a gateway at Hampton Wick. Once through the gate turn right to reach Kingston Bridge and follow the outward path to the Bishop out of Residence.

THAMES PATH - KINGSTON TO SHEPPERTON (9 MILES)

From Kingston the Thames Path ceases to have a dual route and largely follows the towpath. It is on the north bank as far as Hampton Court Bridge and then switches to the south until Shepperton Ferry. For when the ferry is not running (see Walk 7 for times) the Thames Path offers an alternative route over Walton Bridge and through Shepperton village, rejoining the old towpath at Shepperton Lock.

SHEPPERTON
The Kings Head
❧❀❧

This walk takes the ferry across to the south bank of the Thames to allow for a wander around Desborough Island which gives the best view of Shepperton.

The Kings Head – the sign shows Charles I's head – is in a charming village square alongside Thames Cottage and Ye Olde House. It is older than the church opposite which was rebuilt in 1613 with a tower added in the 18th century. The first rector here was appointed in 1271 but the old church had to be demolished after a serious flood caused by the then still tidal Thames.

This 14th-century tavern has a large fireplace in the main panelled and low oak-beamed bar. At the back there is a small bar, where children are welcome, and a conservatory. Entertainment here includes shove-ha'penny, cribbage and dominoes. The inn is well-known for its secret recipe Welsh rarebit and generous helpings of Shepperton Pie which includes melted cheese. Sandwiches can be toasted and baguettes include tuna, prawn, ham or cheese fillings with lettuce and tomato. There are always vegetarian dishes, children's specials and puddings such as treacle tart with lemon ice cream. A changing menu is chalked up on a board in the back bar. Food is served from 12 noon to 2.15 pm and 7.15 pm to 9.45 pm daily except on Sundays. This is a freehouse with a selection of Courage ales. The Kings Head is open from 11 am to 11 pm on Monday to Saturday, and the Sunday hours are 12 noon to 10.30 pm. Telephone: 01932 221910.

- **HOW TO GET THERE:** Shepperton is reached from the A244 and is near junction 1 on the M3. Shepperton station is at the end of the line from Waterloo and Kingston. The Kings Head is in Church Square off Church Road just south of the main shopping street.
- **PARKING:** There is limited parking in Church Square outside the pub and a car park in Church Road.
- **LENGTH OF THE WALK:** 4 miles. Maps: OS Pathfinder 1190 Weybridge, Hampton Court and Esher; OS Landranger 176 West London (inn GR 077666).

THE WALK

First turn right out of the Kings Head to walk along to the river where there is a view of Desborough Island. Old Ferry House next to the church recalls an important crossing here. Behind the church is the rectory, dating from Henry VII's reign, where a curate, J.M. Neale, wrote *Good King Wenceslas*. The external steps at the back of the church lead to the Shepperton Manor pew. After exploring Church Square walk back past the Kings Head and keep ahead along Chertsey Road.

Turn left into Ferry Lane which leads directly to Shepperton Ferry. Ring the bell on the half hour to summon the ferryman from the nearby shop. (The ferry runs at least every hour between 8.30 am and 5 pm with a final run at 5.30 pm; 7.30 pm May to August and 8.30 pm on summer Sundays. Ferry information: 01932 254844.) Apart from a 26 year break to 1986 there has been a ferry here since Henry VI's reign.

On the far side turn left downstream along the towpath to pass D'Oyly Carte Island, once home of Richard D'Oyly Carte whose visitors included William S. Gilbert and Sir Arthur Sullivan. Willow trees at nearby Shepperton inspired the Mikado song *Tit-willow*. Before the bridge was built visitors announced their arrival by ringing the bell at the lychgate by the towpath.

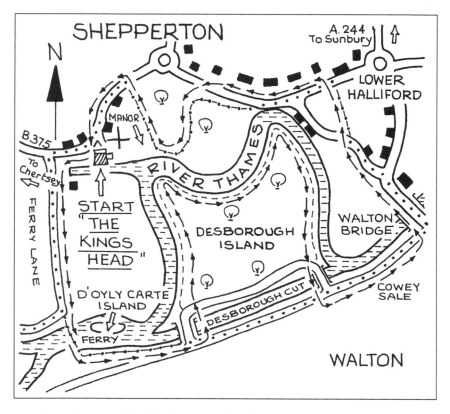

When the river divides there is a bridge. Climb the steps to the right of the towpath arch and go over the Desborough Cut onto Desborough Island, leaving the Thames Path. The 3/4 mile short cut for navigation was only opened in 1935 to avoid the tortuous Shepperton bends.

Once across the bridge go ahead on a path which bears right at the river. The river bank should be on the left. This path is the old towpath and ahead up the water can be seen Shepperton church tower. As the path reaches Point Meadow and bears east there is a view of Shepperton Manor where George Eliot wrote *Scenes of Clerical Life*. Stay by the river – there may be a couple of leaning trees to duck under – and don't be tempted to use the stile. The way is later fenced as the path winds round the island's woodland for about 1/2 mile. On reaching a lodge keep forward up the metalled drive to join a road which climbs up to go over the Cut.

Once across the water at once go left down a flight of steps onto the 'new' towpath. Keep forward downstream where the Old and

New Thames converge. The towpath is alongside Cowey Sale which means 'cows way'. The Thames has probably changed its course here on the floodplain. Walton Bridge ahead, on the site of a ford crossed by Julius Caesar in 54 BC, is still the temporary Bailey bridge erected in 1953. The first was an unusual wooden geometrical design which appears in a Canaletto painting. Walk under the bridge and at once go right to take the steps up onto the approach road to cross the river.

Once back on the Middlesex bank it is possible to see the old bridge approach to the left. Walk down the slope to Windmill Green and cross the road just before the Texaco garage (right). Walk ahead up Walton Lane. This is the Thames Path alternative route for walkers wanting to avoid the ferry or reach Shepperton station.

As the road bears sharp left keep ahead down the right side of a wall by a playing field. At Lower Halliford Green go left past Merlewood House. Over to the right, next to imposing 18th-century Battlecrease House, is Vine Cottage where novelist George Meredith lived. Ahead, marked by a blue plaque, is Peacock House where Thomas Love Peacock, author of the poem *The Genius of the Thames* and father-in-law of Meredith, lived until his death in 1866.

Cross Walton Lane and bear right on the path past the river viewpoint. Go left into Russell Road to pass the Red Lion and the Ship Hotel. From here the Thames Path alternative route is over to the left, set back from the road. Before this path rejoins the road go left over a footbridge crossing the stream to continue parallel to the road. At a junction go left up the approach to Shepperton Cricket Club. Just before the cricket ground go left at a gate to find a path which leads to the riverside. Here there is a fine view of Shepperton Manor. Walk upstream and follow the manor grounds wall to reach Church Road. Go left to reach Church Square and the Kings Head.

THAMES PATH - SHEPPERTON TO ETON (13 MILES)

From Shepperton Ferry the Thames Path is by the lock and on the same north side as far as Staines Bridge. From here the Path is on the south bank to pass along Runnymede to Windsor with only a brief diversion from the towpath to the north side at Datchet to avoid the Windsor Castle private grounds. Eton is reached by way of Windsor Bridge.

ETON
The Waterman's Arms
⌘

Eton is dominated by Henry VI's Eton College whose chapel is seen from various angles on the walk. The route immediately turns up the High Street which, thanks to the College population, still has plenty of small interesting shops, before crossing the riverside playing fields of Eton. The return is by way of two bridges and along the towpath on the edge of Home Park.

Being opposite Eton College Boat House it is not surprising that the Waterman's Arms should have rowing and river pictures on the wall. In the early Eighties there was still an Eton skiff above the bar. This is a small cosy one-bar pub but now there is the Conservatory covering a sheltered yard – two trees grow through the roof – not seen from the narrow Brocas Street which takes its name from Lord Brocas who gave land to Eton College.

The food served in the Conservatory is good value with plenty of sandwiches, salads and omelettes. Seven toppings are offered for the jacket potatoes and ploughman's include a duck pâté version. The long menu of main dishes has such temptations as lemon butterfly chicken, fish and chips and several vegetarian dishes. There is always a choice of puddings. Food in the Conservatory is available from 12 noon to 2 pm daily and 6 pm to 8.45 pm except Sundays. Children are welcome. This is a freehouse with Brakspear Bitter, Courage Best Bitter, Morland Old Speckled Hen, Ruddles County and Wadworth 6X available. The Waterman's Arms is open on Monday to Saturday from 11 am to 2.30 pm and 6 pm to 11 pm. The Sunday hours are 12 noon to 10.30 pm. Telephone: 01753 861001.

- **HOW TO GET THERE:** Eton is just south of Slough. The Waterman's Arms is in Brocas Street just off the south end of Eton High Street. Both Windsor and Eton Riverside station and Windsor Central station are nearby.
- **PARKING:** There is very little parking provision in Eton but Windsor on the opposite side of the river has a large public car park. Note that Windsor Bridge is closed to traffic.
- **LENGTH OF THE WALK:** 3 miles. Maps: OS Pathfinder 1173 Windsor; OS Landranger 175 Reading and Windsor (inn GR 967773).

THE WALK

Turn left out of the Waterman's Arms and walk down Brocas Street to the High Street. Turn left up the High Street where there are likely to be Eton boys in the uniform of black tail coat worn in mourning for George III.

Pass the chapel and main entrance to Eton College. Later there is a long wall to the right. After a short distance note the rungs in the roadside wall used by spectators watching the famous Eton Wall Game held against the far side on or near St Andrew's Day. When the road climbs over a stream, known as The Jordan, look back to see an impressive view of the chapel built in the 15th century as just the east end choir of an intended larger building. Later look down to see the milestone indicating one mile to Windsor Guildhall.

Here turn right through a kissing-gate by the Upper Club cricket pavilion. Go forward on the path to bear round to the right to a bridge spanning The Jordan. Do not cross the bridge but turn round and take the right-hand path away from the bridge. The Thames is over to the right.

At the far end cross a stream and go right inside a fence by a road. Immediately beyond Boathouse Cottage go right to leave the road by a

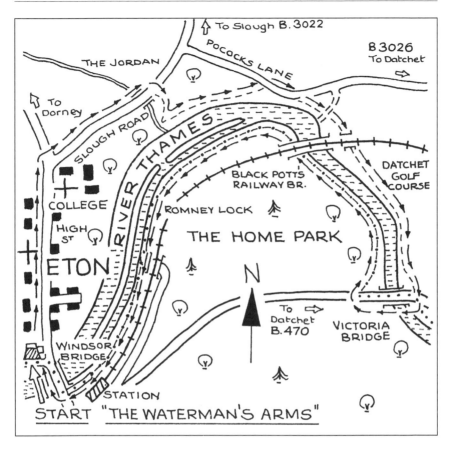

short metalled drive leading to a boathouse. Walk in front of the boathouse to find a stile. Keep forward over rough ground to a traditional stile and a squeeze stile taking the path over the Black Pott's driveway into another field. The path direction is forward over a field, crossing a bridge on the way, to reach a kissing-gate before the railway bridge.

Pass under the low tunnel of Black Pott's railway bridge and follow a short path ahead to the grounds of Datchet Golf Club. Keep forward by the trees to the right. Later there is a firm path underfoot which serves as an access for the houseboats on the river to the right. As soon as the river has disappeared look to the right for steps, beyond a ditch. Take these steps up to a road and turn right. The pavement runs up onto Victoria Bridge which was designed by Prince Albert but given a new span in 1967 – there is a twin called Albert downstream.

● The Thames Path from Datchet joins here. Its route downstream
  provides a fine view of the private section of Home Park and the
Royal Boathouse.

Cross the bridge and at the end of the railing on the right go right
with the Thames Path to join the towpath. Continue upstream with
good views of Windsor Castle on high ground. On the far bank,
immediately before Black Pott's railway bridge, is the successor to a
fishing lodge used by both Charles II and Izaak Walton of *Compleat
Angler* fame.

Pass under the railway bridge. The river bank, rich in wildflowers in
summer, has a view of Eton's playing fields beyond an island. At a
kissing-gate go through a boatyard to a lane. Soon there is a view of
Eton College Chapel. Turn right off the main path into the narrow
Romney Walk which leads to the Donkey House pub. Continue ahead
to climb the steps to Windsor Bridge and cross the river. Once on the
Eton bank go left into Brocas Street to reach the Waterman's Arms.

● **THAMES PATH - ETON TO MEDMENHAM (15 MILES)**

The Thames Path runs past the Waterman's Arms and on to The Brocas.
There is no crossing until Maidenhead Bridge. A detour just before
Cookham means that the river is regained at the village church. The
Path returns to the north bank by way of Bourne End railway bridge. A
diversion from the water in Marlow is part of the historic towpath. At
Temple a bridge erected for the Thames Path has replaced a disused
ferry to allow the Path to pass Medmenham on the opposite bank
which affords the best view of the Abbey. Medmenham itself can be
reached by way of the Harleyford Estate, via the Temple Lock approach
road and a tunnel beneath a clifftop garden.

MEDMENHAM
The Dog & Badger

The outward route of this walk is past the church and down Ferry Lane to find the river flowing past the mysterious Medmenham Abbey. The towpath stretch on this walk is rare as it is not incorporated into the official Thames Path which, due to loss of ferries, has to take the opposite bank. However, the Medmenham bank affords the best views of the Culham Court mansion and illustrates how the curving Thames can play tricks with one's sense of direction.

The Dog & Badger is a long, low-beamed, 14th-century roadside inn. There is one bar under a roof of tankards near the fireplace. The decorations include plenty of shiny horsebrasses. On the wall in a dark corner is a history of the church opposite which once owned the building. Until 1899 banns of marriage used to be read in the pub as well as the church. A Roundhead cannon ball was discovered here during building work and a Restoration customer was Nell Gwynne. In the following century members of the notorious and allegedly blasphemous Hell Fire Club were among the patrons.

Food is a major feature and two menu boards are propped up by a window. Ploughman's lunches come with Cheddar, Stilton or pâté. Jumbo sausage or scampi is accompanied by chips and peas. There is usually soup and baguettes can be served with fries. Sunday lunch is popular here with families coming from nearby Marlow and Henley. This is a Whitbread house offering Brakspear, Wadworth and Flowers ales. The Dog & Badger is open from 11 am to 3 pm and 5.30 pm to 11 pm on weekdays and the Sunday hours are 12 noon to 3 pm and 7 pm to 10.30 pm. Food is available at lunchtime and in the evening until 10 pm except on Sunday evening. Telephone: 01491 571362.

- **HOW TO GET THERE:** Medmenham is on the A4155, between Henley and Marlow.
- **PARKING:** There is a car park at the Dog & Badger.
- **LENGTH OF THE WALK:** 3$1/2$ miles. Maps: OS Explorer 3 Chiltern Hills South; OS Landranger 175 Reading and Windsor (inn GR 804845).

THE WALK

Cross the road and turn left to the road junction. Go right down Ferry Lane. There is an entrance to the churchyard at the end of the wall. Continue down the road, passing a footpath to the right, just before The Manor House, which is part of the return route.

Beyond a bridge the road is alongside Medmenham Abbey. This was a Cistercian foundation begun in 1201 and closed in 1536 when the community had dwindled to an abbot and one monk. The attractive ruins, best seen from the river, became a meeting place for Sir Francis Dashwood's Hell Fire Club between 1750 and 1774. Members were known as 'Franciscans of Medmenham'.

The lane runs directly to Medmenham Ferry. Go over the footbridge to join the towpath which has crossed from the Berkshire bank opposite. The ferry has ceased to run but there is an impressive monument recalling a famous court case in 1899 which declared the ferry to be for public use. Charles II, a friend of Nell Gwynne, crossed here and after the judgment Edward VII and later George V, accompanied by Queen Mary, used the ferry.

Go through the Conservancy gate and stay by the river on the towpath. The Thames Path is on the opposite bank. There may be a collapsed Conservancy gate further on. At a third gate there is a view to

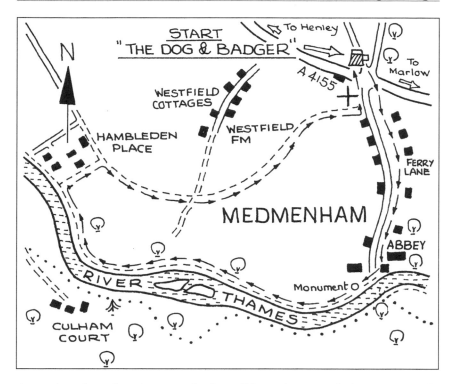

the right of a white house which will later be revealed as a riverside residence. Before the towpath has curved round to this point it passes beneath the high standing Culham Court on the far bank. The mansion was built in 1770 in the reign of George III who stayed at the new house. By the 20th century it was the home of Lady Barber, who founded Birmingham's Barber Institute of Fine Arts in 1932. Banker and arts patron Michael Behrens followed and his choice of modern sculpture can still be seen dotted around the gardens.

The path runs up to a large Conservancy gate leading into the garden of the whitewashed house. Whilst the towpath continues through the garden the public footpath turns right and inland up the side of the house, following the hedge. On reaching a couple of stiles at the end of a lane (left) turn sharp right to roughly follow a line of poles.

The path veers to the left of the brick building ahead where there is a (probably broken) stile. Cross a concrete farm road and go over the second stile to head for a third one on the far side of the field. Go over another concrete access road flanked by stiles and keep forward to the line of trees ahead. Beyond the trees there is a junction. Take the left-hand path and bear left over to the field boundary which is followed round the corner. Keep by the left-hand edge of the field to reach the northern corner where there is a stile.

Cross a concrete road and go over a stile by a gate. Keep ahead along the side of the field (left) to go over a couple of stiles in the trees ahead. The way is now forward to reach steps leading up to Ferry Lane at Medmenham. Go left to reach the church and crossroads. The Dog & Badger is to the left.

 ### THAMES PATH - MEDMENHAM TO ASTON (3½ MILES)

From the Temple footbridge the Thames Path is on the south bank as far as Aston with only a simple diversion from the riverside as the Path passes through the Culham Court grounds.

ASTON
The Flower Pot
❧

This walk leaves the little hamlet to follow the towpath on its long curve to Remenham church, passing both the riverside home of W.H. Smith and Temple Island with its folly fishing lodge. Nearer still, at Hambleden Lock, it is possible to walk across a long weir to enjoy the views. The return is by way of a hill giving a view across to the Chilterns.

This Victorian boating pub has 'good accommodation for fishing and boating parties' painted on the outside and a large flower pot in a bracket overhanging the road. There are two bars with old Thames prints on the walls, a dartboard, real books and even a newspaper. The large garden with plenty of seats is inhabited by chickens. Accommodation is still offered but the 1893 boast of 'boatman always in attendance' no longer holds – indeed Ferry Lane now leads only to a disused ferry.

The food includes substantial sandwiches and home-made dishes.

The breakfast served in summer from 8 am to 10 am is popular with those who have slept overnight on a boat. This is a Brakspear tied house offering the local beer from upstream Henley where brewing has taken place on the same site for at least 300 years. The opening hours are 11 am to 3 pm and 6 pm to 11 pm on Monday to Saturday, 12 noon to 3 pm and 7 pm to 10.30 pm on Sunday, with food available from 12 noon to 2 pm and 6.30 pm to 9 pm except on Sunday nights. Telephone: 01491 574721.

- **HOW TO GET THERE:** Aston is north of Remenham Hill on the A4130 Henley-Hurley road. Nearby Mill End, across the Hambleden weir, is served by buses from Henley.
- **PARKING:** There is a car park opposite the Flower Pot.
- **LENGTH OF THE WALK:** 3 miles. Maps: OS Explorer 3 Chiltern Hills South; OS Landranger 175 Reading and Windsor (inn GR 784843).

THE WALK

Turn left out of the pub to walk north down Ferry Lane. On the right, by the Victorian postbox, is the Old Post Office. A little further on is Ferry Cottage on the left and Ferry House on the right. The lane leads directly to the old ferry point where the towpath crosses.

Turn left over a footbridge and through a kissing-gate. The mill stream can be seen flowing into the river on the far side. At the end of the field go through a gate and join the rough track leading to Hambleden Lock. Soon there is a view across to Hambleden Mill. A 300 yard narrow public footpath runs across the weir from the lock to the mill which was working until 1955 having been in existence since the 13th century.

Beyond the lock the towpath is over grass for only a very short distance before the hard surface, running all the way to Henley, begins. Soon there is a good view across the water to the dazzling white Greenlands mansion, once home of newsagent and bookseller W.H. Smith and now Henley Management College. Continue to bear south with the river below the Chiltern Hills on the far bank represented by the dramatic beechwoods of Fawley and Hambleden. Ahead in the river is Temple Island, sometimes called Regatta Island because of its association with the annual Henley Royal Regatta in July. The island once belonged to Fawley Court (upstream on the far bank) and the island's fishing lodge, designed in 1771 by James Wyatt, was intended as a focus for a vista from the mansion.

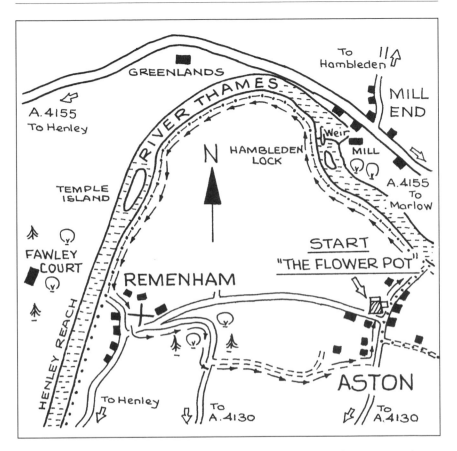

On coming to a house look for a turning inland to Remenham, leaving the Thames Path. Go through the kissing-gate and up the road to the church which is Victorian although there was a Norman church on the site. On the north-east side of the churchyard, by a huge angel, is the tomb of 18th-century Hambleden lock-keeper Caled Gould, an ancestor of politician Bryan Gould.

Turn left at the lychgate to walk up the road on the far side of the church. At the next junction go right to follow a road which runs uphill and round a bend. Continue along the flat for a short distance to find a stile by gates on the left.

Turn left over the stile and follow the track ahead across the open country. After 300 yards there is a copse to the right. Later the way climbs to become tree lined as the ground rises to afford views to the north. At the bend keep forward into a sloping field and go down to a stile. Beyond is a path which meets a road by the entrance to Highway Cottage at Aston. Turn left along Aston Lane to pass Wisteria Cottage on the right. Ahead is the Flower Pot.

THAMES PATH - ASTON TO READING (10 MILES)

From Remenham, on this walk, the Thames Path runs directly to Henley Bridge where the Path continues on the north side. There is a diversion at Shiplake and at Sonning the Path returns to the south side on its way to Reading.

CAVERSHAM
The Three Men in a Boat Tavern

❦

This walk begins in Reading but immediately crosses the river to explore the view seen from the pub. After passing through a churchyard, the way is up onto The Mount to visit an old well before descending into the town to find an Edwardian church which incorporates ancient Thames stones. The return is along the towpath on the Reading side passing a unique bowls club.

The Three Men in a Boat Tavern seems an unlikely Thames pub, being a modern building and part of a Holiday Inn complex. It is also unfortunate that Jerome K. Jerome's book *Three Men in a Boat* is rather rude about the town: 'One does not linger in the neighbourhood of Reading.' However, the pub does have a fine view of Caversham

Bridge and Caversham church in the trees on the far bank, and the river outside is often white with swans. This new pub is a successor to the White Hart which had been built on the site of the pre-Reformation Holy Ghost Chapel.

The pub's interior is a little like a boathouse with oars and old Thames photographs on the walls. It even has an advertisement from *The Bystander* in 1913 depicting Johnnie Walker enjoying boating at Windsor. There is plenty of space and large windows exploit the fine view which can also be enjoyed from the terrace where the pub cat is often to be found.

Ham, cheese, tuna and turkey are served as fillings for sandwiches and baguettes which come with salad garnish and potato crisps. There are also main dishes and baskets of chips. Steamed puddings are listed on a board. Another board above the bar has a list of the week's guest beers. The Three Men in a Boat Tavern is open during the week from 12 noon to 2.30 pm (3 pm on Saturday) and 5.30 pm to 11 pm, and on Sunday from 12 noon to 3.30 pm and 7 pm to 10.30 pm. It opens all day in summer. Food is available at lunchtimes to 2 pm (3 pm Sunday) and in the evenings except Saturday until 9.30 pm. Telephone: 01734 259988.

- **HOW TO GET THERE:** The Three Men in a Boat is on the Reading (south) bank of the river, next to Caversham Bridge which is part of the A4155 Reading-Henley road.
- **PARKING:** There is a large car park in the adjoining Holiday Inn.
- **LENGTH OF THE WALK:** 3 miles. Maps: Reading Estate Publications Street Map; OS Pathfinder 1172 Reading; OS Landranger 175 Reading and Windsor (inn GR 712746).

THE WALK

Leave the pub by the river entrance and turn right downstream along the towpath to go up onto Caversham Bridge. The first bridge was built about 1219 by Reading Abbey to improve the Oxford road route. On the downstream side, where the bridge crossed an island, there was St Anne's Chapel which housed the statue of Our Lady of Caversham and some noted Holy Land relics. It had almost the same status as the Shrine of Our Lady of Walsingham in Norfolk and the many Royal pilgrims to Caversham included Catherine of Aragon whose husband, Henry VIII, closed both bridge chapels in 1538. The Holy Ghost Chapel, on the pub site, was demolished and St Anne's on the bridge survived for a few

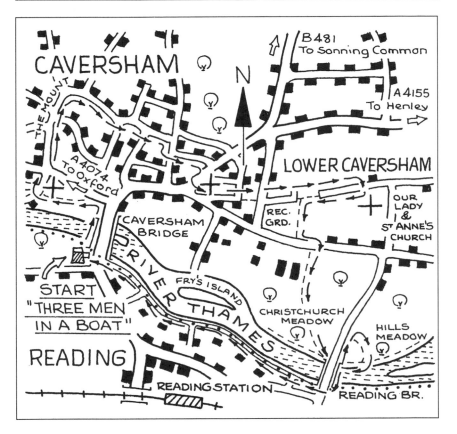

years as a converted house. Stone from the base of the bridge's chapel is now incorporated into Our Lady of Caversham Chapel, visited later.

Cross the river to walk from Reading to Caversham and go ahead up Bridge Street. At the traffic lights turn left into Church Road. Stay on the left-hand side to pass The Rectory – a recent rector dived daily into the Thames every summer for 20 years.

Immediately after the double bend bear left away from the road into the churchyard where a path runs uphill past the partly Norman church which, like St Anne's Chapel, was under the jurisdiction of Notley Abbey in Buckinghamshire. At a road go right to walk up to a junction on St Peter's Hill. Go between the barriers opposite to climb a steep path known as The Mount. Before reaching a gate look over the wall on the right to see a dramatic drop. Beyond the gate stay ahead but walk on the right side of the road and ignore all turnings as The Mount bears round to the right to become Priest Hill.

Cross the top of St Anne's Road to find the Holy Well of St Anne which drops 80 feet to the level of the Thames. Follow Priest Hill downhill to Hemdean Road and turn right to go left into Chester Street. Above a corner shop at the far end there is an old painted notice advertising 'Corn, Hay, Straw, Meal and Offal'.

Cross Prospect Street to Caversham post office and turn right. At a junction by a church go left into South Street. At the far end continue ahead along a narrow passage leading to Westfield Road. Cross straight over to go ahead up Falkland Road. Stay on the right to continue on a footpath alongside a recreation ground.

The path leads directly to the end of South View Avenue where there is the brick church of Our Lady and St Anne dating from 1902. The dedication recalls the bridge chapel. This Edwardian church has a Norman style shrine chapel built onto its north-east corner. Incorporated in this 1958 addition are stones from the foundations of the bridge chapel which were discovered in 1924 during the building of the present Caversham Bridge. A squint allows visitors to see a 500 year old statue of Our Lady.

Retrace the footpath for a short distance and go left into Westfield Recreation Ground. Follow the path ahead along the edge to the main road on the far side. Go through the park gateway which is almost opposite. Walk ahead on the straight metalled path to a bridge over a stream. Still continue ahead over the grass of Christchurch Meadow. This open ground was once a wide marsh which, along with the Thames, separated the Oxfordshire village of Caversham from Reading. After passing a tennis court bear left onto a metalled path running towards a path junction by Reading Bridge.

Go under the bridge and after a short distance turn left on a path which runs up to the road. Turn left to walk over the bridge which has a view downstream of Caversham Lock. Once on the Reading side go down steps to join the towpath and turn left under the bridge.

The towpath passes a crane on the Thames Conservancy Wharf – now the Environment Agency's Thames Navigation and Recreation headquarters. Later there is a terrace of houses which includes the Thames House Hotel. Here a ferry runs across to Fry's Island where there is the only bowls club in Britain reached by ferry. It is known locally as De Montford Island after a duel fought there in 1163 between Robert de Montford and Henry, Earl of Essex, in the presence of Henry II. De Montfort had accused Essex of dropping the Royal Standard during battle. In the duel watched by thousands Essex fell and his body

Our Lady of Caversham Chapel.

was taken to Reading Abbey where he recovered and joined the community.

After Caversham Wharf there is the Riverside Restaurant and Wine Bar on the site of Salter's Boatyard. Continue ahead under Caversham Bridge to the Three Men in a Boat.

THAMES PATH - READING TO SOUTH STOKE (10½ MILES)

The Thames Path continues from the Three Men in a Boat on the south bank as far as Tilehurst where there is a complicated but waymarked diversion through a housing estate and back to the Thames at Mapledurham Lock. At Pangbourne the Path moves to the north bank to have its only climb – up the Whitchurch main street and through woods to join the towpath below Gatehampton railway bridge. At Goring the Path crosses the river whilst the Ridgeway national trail provides a direct path to South Stoke on the opposite (north) bank.

SOUTH STOKE
The Perch and Pike

South Stoke is a quiet, unspoilt village with church, shop and pub, the latter perfectly placed for the start of a short exploration of the towpath on the east side of the Thames. Because of the loss of the ancient ferries, the Thames Path itself is on the west side of the river, as far as Wallingford. This is a shame because the walking is much better on the other side along here, which is why I have selected South Stoke for the start of a walk beside this section of the Thames.

This pub is like a cottage by the side of the road in a village which is still free of through traffic. But in recent years many have made their way here for the delicious food. Outside the Perch and Pike there is a splendid old sign attached to the wall – an indication of a really old pub – depicting fish. Inside are two rooms, both with fireplaces where real logs burn in winter. There are books and two papers on rods to read. The bar in one of the rooms is almost hidden behind old woodwork.

The menu is extensive and all food is served at the tables where linen napkins are laid. The traditional sandwiches or ploughman's are available but visitors are often tempted by the ever changing menu on the large board. Soup might be bean, pea and mint and served piping hot in a large white tureen with French style bread and butter. Propped up on the books is a small board with a long list of puddings. This is a Brakspear house with real ale. The Perch and Pike is open on Monday to Saturday from 12 noon to 2 pm and 6 pm to 11 pm. Sunday opening is from 12 noon to 3 pm and 7 pm to 10.30 pm. Food is served all the time except on Sunday evenings. Telephone: 01491 872415.

- **HOW TO GET THERE:** South Stoke is signposted off the B4009 just north of Goring in Oxfordshire.
- **PARKING:** There is a car park at the Perch and Pike.
- **LENGTH OF THE WALK:** 3 miles. Maps: OS Pathfinder 1155 Wantage (East) and Didcot (South) and OS Explorer 3 Chiltern Hills South; OS Landranger 174 Newbury and Wantage and 175 Reading and Windsor (inn GR 598836).

THE WALK

Turn right out of the pub forecourt to walk along the village street. The church is 13th-century with much 14th-century alteration including the doors and the statue niches. On the north side there is a wall painting and in the chancel an imposing monument to Dr Griffith Higgs, chaplain to the Queen of Bohemia, Charles I's sister.

Continue along the road to the junction and bear left round the Corner House to pass between College Farm House and the Old Forge House. At the next junction, by Ashmount House, go left again. The lane leads directly to the old Moulsford Ferry which occasionally operates in the summer.

Across the water is the Beetle and Wedge pub named after the mallet once used on the site for driving a wedge into logs for splitting before being floated downstream. Bernard Shaw often stayed there when the landlord ran the ferry. The pub features in *Three Men in a Boat*. Here at 'Mouls-ford' the last time farm carts forded was in the 1890s.

Turn upstream through the gate on the towpath which has crossed from the far side leaving the modern Thames Path to run behind the waterside village. Soon there is a good view of the whitewashed Manor House, home of publisher Robert Maxwell's son Kevin and his family. Their baby daughter was christened at the next door church on the Sunday after his famous trial ended in his acquittal. Upstream, beyond

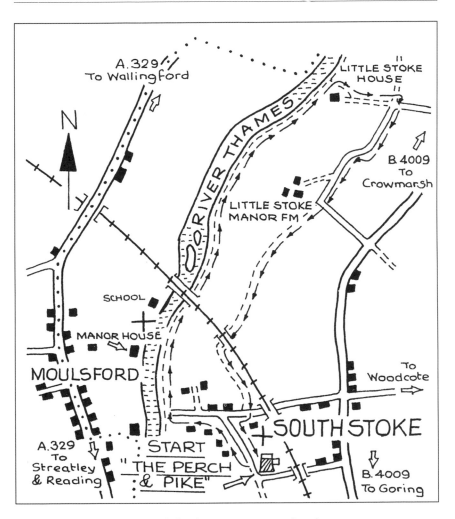

the boatyard, is the Moulsford Preparatory School.

Beyond the village the towpath runs under Moulsford railway bridge, built to a Brunel design in 1838-9. The upstream section, also with interesting brickwork, was added in 1892 to accommodate extra tracks.

Pass through a gate and keep across a small field to a footbridge and a second gate. Further on another Conservancy gate is level with the inland buildings of Littlestoke Manor Farm. Later there is a redundant iron gate before yet another Conservancy gate. After a bridge over a stream, the path is narrow as it runs to the old Little Stoke Ferry which takes the towpath back to the other bank. Papist Way, part of the

Thames Path, can be seen running down from Fair Mile Hospital on the far bank.

Turn inland to a junction and pass between Ferry Cottage on the left and then Little Stoke House on the right. The gravel drive bears round to the right with a high brick wall to reach a thatched barn. Go left along the road to a junction and turn right.

After 1/4 mile the road passes Littlestoke Manor Farm. At the sharp turn left go ahead across the entrance to Littlestoke Manor and over a stone stile under a beech tree. Keep straight ahead along the side of a field to reach a footbridge at the far end. Continue forward on the path which gently veers to the left and enters another field to cut its corner. Go through a long, narrow tunnel under the railway. On the far side go left on a path which soon gently bears over to the opposite side of the field to slip behind a fence and pass two cottages on the edge of South Stoke. Keep ahead along the short lane to a junction by November Cottage. Ahead is Manor Farm which has a 17th-century dovecot. Go right towards the Corner House and bear left to pass the church and return to the Perch and Pike.

THAMES PATH - SOUTH STOKE TO WALLINGFORD (2 MILES)

South Stoke is on the Ridgeway national trail which runs north out of Goring. At Little Stoke Ferry the Ridgeway continues alongside the Thames and through North Stoke and Mongewell Park to join Walk 13 at the tunnel under the Wallingford bypass.

WALK 13

WALLINGFORD
The George Hotel

❦

Wallingford, meaning 'Welsh people's ford', is on the ancient London road and it was here that William the Conqueror crossed the Thames in 1066 on his long journey from Hastings to be crowned in Westminster Abbey. Next year he ordered the building of the castle where later Chaucer's son was Constable. The walk crosses the Thames to visit the meadows, with a view of Wallingford's famous candle snuffer church spire and bridge, before passing lonely Newnham Murren church. The return is by way of a new Thames bridge opened in 1993, then north along the towpath and through the old town.

The George is in Wallingford's High Street and dates from 1517 when Geoffrey and Elizabeth Bayton opened a new inn called the George and Dragon. Being in the shadow of Wallingford Castle it is not surprising that the inn was caught up in the Civil War. The now ruined castle was under siege from the Roundheads in 1646 and at the inn Royalist sergeant John Hobson was stabbed to death during a brawl. The distraught landlord's daughter, seeing her fiancé killed, locked herself in a room for days and with her tears and soot from the fire painted large teardrops on the wall which survive today. The bedroom is now known as the Teardrop Room.

The Long Tavern Barn, running from the front of the building to a very large fireplace at the back, is popular with locals. Here bar meals include Vienna batons with such fillings as coronation chicken or ham. There is a choice of ten fillings for jacket potatoes and Ploughman's Platter features Stilton and baked ham. The George is a Courage house with Directors ale available. The Long Tavern is open from 10 am to 2.30 pm and 6 pm to 11 pm during the week and the Sunday hours are 12 noon to 3 pm and 7 pm to 10.30 pm. Food is served from 12 noon to 2 pm except on Sundays. Coffee or hot chocolate with doughnuts and cakes are available from 10 am every day. Telephone: 01491 836665.

- **HOW TO GET THERE:** Wallingford is on the A4130 between Henley and Didcot. The nearest station is Cholsey & Moulsford, on the Paddington to Didcot line, served by buses from Wallingford.
- **PARKING:** There is a car park at the George but the entrance is in Castle Street.
- **LENGTH OF THE WALK:** 2 miles. Maps: OS Explorer 3 Chiltern Hills South; OS Landranger 175 Reading and Windsor (inn GR 608896).

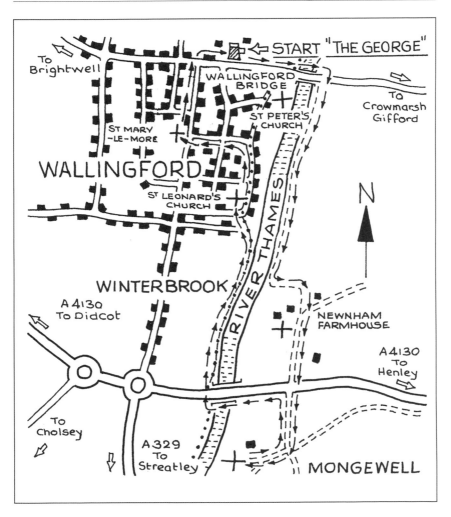

Map showing: To Brightwell, START "THE GEORGE", WALLINGFORD BRIDGE, To Crowmarsh Gifford, ST PETER'S CHURCH, ST MARY -LE-MORE, WALLINGFORD, ST LEONARD'S CHURCH, RIVER THAMES, N, WINTERBROOK, A4130 To Didcot, NEWNHAM FARMHOUSE, A4130 To Henley, To Cholsey, A329 To Streatley, MONGEWELL

THE WALK

At the George's archway entrance turn left along the High Street to reach Wallingford's 800 ft long bridge dating from 1141. The structure has been patched up many times – the Norman stone found towards the Crowmarsh side came from the Priory which stood on the site of the museum in the High Street until Henry VIII's reign. Stay on the left to cross the water and at once go left down steps on the upstream side.

At the bottom go left under the archway and through a gate to follow the towpath. This is the official towpath with at once a view of Wallingford's other great landmark – St Peter's church and its fine spire.

The first church was destroyed in the Civil War and a century later leading lawyer Sir William Blackstone, who wrote *Commentaries on the Laws of England* and is buried in St Peter's, was largely responsible for the rebuilding and for commissioning Sir Robert Taylor's slender spire. There is also a fine view of Wallingford's Thames Street gardens.

Continue along the river, using the footbridges with kissing-gates. Beyond the boatyard on the far bank, the towpath officially moves to the opposite bank for this is the site of Wallingford Lock which existed only from 1838 to 1883 and was used only at times of very low water. Jerome in *Three Men in a Boat* is confused when in about 1888 he fails to find the lock he knew. A ferry started after the lock closed has ceased to run.

Just before coming level with the farm buildings over to the left, turn sharp left inland to walk towards a lonely waymark post. Once at the post go right to a kissing-gate and ahead first over rough ground and then a concrete surface to a stile.

Turn right along the track to pass Newnham Farmhouse and Newnham Murren church. Newnham means 'newly settled place' and 'Murren' comes from lord of the manor Richard Moren who altered the little Norman church in the 1260s. It was again restored in 1849 leaving the Norman entrance and chancel arch. Inside, on the south wall, there is a memorial brass pierced by a stray bullet fired during the siege of Wallingford Castle. Beyond the church the path narrows to a rough tree-lined way. The ground is paved on approaching a tunnel where there is a choice of route.

To visit the ruined church at Mongewell, continue ahead under Wallingford bypass. Keep on along a straight paved path to reach buildings. Here bear right over to the Carmel College notice where a waymark points to the church. Follow the college road and where the way divides go right as indicated by a yellow landmark. On reaching a house ahead go left to find the church beyond a gate in the trees. The chancel dates from the Norman period whilst the tower was added by Bishop Shute Barrington of Durham who held the Mongewell estate in the late 18th and early 19th centuries. The mansion has gone and the grounds are occupied by Carmel College which is a Jewish school – visitors should remember that on Saturdays the college community is observing the Sabbath. Retrace the route back to go under the bypass and turn left.

The main walk from Newnham Murren church continues to the right, before the tunnel, to run round the corner and join the pavement of the

Market Place, Wallingford.

bypass. Continue over the river and once on the far side turn right down a zig-zag path to the towpath on the upstream side of the bridge. Do not go under the bridge but turn left upstream towards Wallingford. Soon the towpath leaves the meadow to become enclosed at the point where the lock was located. The weir was on this side just below Bradford's Brook. Here a Thames Conservancy house close to the path has flood marks for 1894, 1947 and 1979. Continue over a boatyard and round a bend to Lower Wharf. At once turn right to go under an archway in a house – note the 1894 floodmark on the right – and over the mill stream. The path runs behind the east end of Wallingford's St Leonard's church. This, Wallingford's oldest church with Norman origins, was used as a barracks by Cromwell's troops during the siege of the castle.

Turn right along Thames Street to pass Riverside where artist George Dunlop Leslie RA lived from 1884 to 1907 – he painted the angels in St Leonard's. Cromwell Lodge, also on the right, is where Oliver Cromwell is alleged to have stayed. When the doors of Wallingford Rowing Club are open there is a glimpse of the river. Ahead is the entrance to Castle Priory, built in 1759 as the home of Sir William Blackstone. The road has a bend here because Sir William extended his garden.

Immediately after the double bend go left through a doorway and along the side of a car park. At Wood Street go right and at once left into Hart Street. At St Mary's Street turn right to pass Boots and enter the Market Place. The Town Hall, built in 1670, hides St Mary-le-More which has a tower almost certainly built of stones from the demolished castle. The curfew is rung from here daily at 9 pm. Keep forward to continue along the northern end of St Mary Street which is closed to traffic. At the High Street go right to reach the George on the left.

THAMES PATH - WALLINGFORD TO DORCHESTER (5 MILES)

The Thames Path runs north from the bridge, at the east end of Wallingford High Street, to cross the river at the Preston Crowmarsh Lock. The way then stays on the north bank past Shillingford Bridge to run up the attractive main street and briefly join a main road before returning to the towpath which crosses the mouth of the river Thame at Dorchester.

DORCHESTER
The George Hotel
❧❧❧

Dorchester is a former Roman town dominated by a 12th-century abbey church which replaced a Saxon cathedral. The abbey, visited on this walk, has a 14th-century wall painting, a sculptured Jesse window and the restored shrine of St Birinus, the founder of the cathedral. The route continues to the confluence of the rivers Thame and Thames before following the latter upstream to Little Wittenham where the annual Pooh sticks competition is held.

The nearby abbey had a brewhouse on the site of the George as early as 1140. The present inn is a building dating from around 1449 – almost a century before Henry VIII closed the monastery. Situated in the High Street, it was later an important coaching inn for London-Oxford travellers as the abandoned coach outside reminds us. Inside the inn there is a room said to be haunted by a white lady who appears at the end of a four-poster bed.

As may be expected the bar has beams and a fireplace with real logs burning in winter. There are several old photographs of the Thames and nearby Day's Lock. Recent copies of *Country Life* are on one of the old oak tables for those drinking alone. Food available at lunchtimes includes home-made soup. The open sandwiches are substantial – bacon, lettuce and tomato comes with salad and even roast potatoes. The puddings list always includes sticky toffee pudding served with toffee sauce and clotted cream. There are also main dishes such as steak and ale pie and a roast lunch on Sundays. This is a freehouse with Brakspear, Morland and guest beers and an exceptionally wide choice of wine by the glass. The George is open every weekday from 11 am to 11 pm and the Sunday hours are 12 noon to 10.30 pm. Food is available from 12 noon to 2 pm and 7 pm to 9.30 pm. Telephone: 01865 340404.

● **HOW TO GET THERE:** Dorchester is just off the A423 between Maidenhead and Oxford. The London-Oxford coaches (Thames Transit 390) stop in the main street.

● **PARKING:** There is a car park at the George.

● **LENGTH OF THE WALK:** 3 miles. Maps: OS Pathfinder 1136 Abingdon; OS Landranger 164 Oxford (inn GR 578943).

THE WALK

Turn right out of the George and cross the road to enter the grounds of the abbey church. Leave the church by the south porch and keep ahead down the path to a gate by the toll-house where tolls were collected from 1815 until 1873. Bear left and just before the bridge go left to find a hidden path which runs down to a tunnel. Once through the low passage turn left to pass the Roman Catholic church which is appropriately dedicated to St Birinus. The architect of the church, completed in 1849, was Pugin admirer William Wilkinson Wardell who emigrated to Australia where he designed Melbourne Cathedral.

Continue ahead along the right side of the green. Keep forward but before reaching a thatched cottage ahead go sharp right under a barrier and up a short path. At the end go left and where the way divides keep forward (but not directly ahead) on a footpath running down the side of a field. Go over a wooden stile at the end to continue south. Stay near the field boundary to the left to bear round the corner of the oddly shaped field and find a stile ahead. Still continue forward to meet the river Thame at a bend and follow the bank to its confluence with the Thames. This meeting of waters, according to some, marks the place

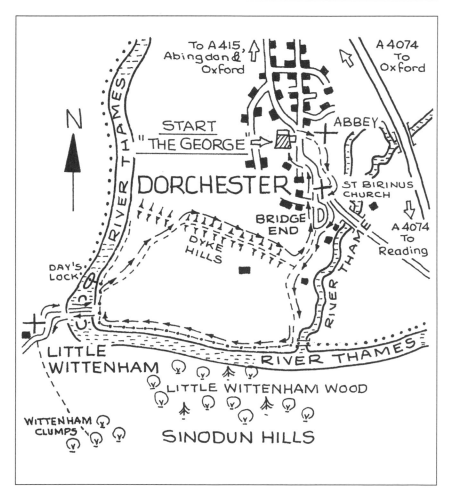

where the Thames becomes the Isis – Oxford's name for the river.

Turn right to walk upstream along the towpath with Little Wittenham Wood, a nature reserve, on the far bank, where at least 120 species of birds have been recorded. After a gate the path is fenced off from the river. At a second gate, a traditional Thames Conservancy gate with a carved number, the path is unfenced as the Thames turns north to go under the bridge leading to Little Wittenham.

To visit Little Wittenham cross the bridge over the main navigation channel and go across the island, with the lock-keeper's house, to walk over the far channel. The first bridge is the scene of the annual World Pooh Sticks Championships held at noon on the first Sunday in January.

The path leads to a lane which climbs up to Little Wittenham's church which has a 15th-century tower. Its correct name of Wittenham Abbots is derived from its connection with upstream Abingdon Abbey. Opposite is a path leading up to Wittenham Clumps – beech trees in an Iron Age fort – on top of the Sinodun Hills. The local name is 'Mother Daunch's Buttocks', recalling Oliver Cromwell's aunt, Marie Dunch, who lived at the Manor House next to the church. (Her figure can be seen laid out below the tower in the church.) From the viewpoint there are views of the Chilterns in the east, the Berkshire Downs in the south and Didcot Power Station in the west as well as the Thames below.

Retrace the lane back to the towpath. A short distance upstream, reached on the Thames Path, is Day's Lock which is named after an 1820s lock-keeper.

To continue the pub walk, go through the gate by the bridge and bear half left across the field towards Dorchester Abbey in the distance. Pass through a wooden gate and follow an enclosed footpath which soon cuts through the Iron Age earthworks, known as Dyke Hills, to run along their north side. At the far end the path joins the outward route. On approaching Dorchester keep forward up Wittenham Lane to reach the Chequers which is opposite St Birinus' church. Walk ahead to Dorchester's High Street and the George.

THAMES PATH - DORCHESTER TO CLIFTON HAMPDEN (2½ MILES)

From Day's Lock, just north of the bridge at Little Wittenham, the Thames Path is on the south bank as far as Clifton Hampden.

CLIFTON HAMPDEN
The Barley Mow

Clifton Hampden is a village of tea cosy cottages. The design for the elegant brick bridge was sketched on a shirt cuff by George Gilbert Scott who was called in by Lord Aldenham after he inherited the village in 1842. His nieces collected tolls in person from the toll-house until 1946. This walk crosses the river to explore the length of the Thames' Clifton Cut on the towpath which offers a fine view, looking back, of the bridge. The return is by way of the thatched village.

'It is without exception, I should say, the quaintest, most old-world inn up the river' according to Jerome K. Jerome writing in *Three Men in a Boat*. More than a century on the Barley Mow still has the 'story-book appearance' he reported. The inn was built in 1352 as the date on the outside wall indicates. This was 150 years before there was a ferry link with the village on the opposite bank. The bridge was opened in 1864. The pub has very low beams in the stone floored bar and the cosy flanking rooms. Old engravings are on the walls although opposite the servery there are pictures of the fire in 1975 which nearly brought disaster. The garden has rustic seats and even a boat on the lawn.

The usual ploughman's is always on offer, as well as soup – maybe thick vegetable with tarragon – and a vegetarian dish. But the menu often includes steak and ale pie and a roast. In the evenings you will find steak or fish with peas and chips and Thai dishes. There are also two or three puddings. 'Barley Mow' means 'barley stack', barley being an important ingredient of beer, and this Chef and Brewer house has Courage real ales. The Barley Mow is open from 11 am to 2.30 pm and 6 pm to 11 pm on weekdays and the Sunday hours are 12 noon to 3 pm and 7 pm to 10.30 pm. Food is available from 12 noon to 2 pm (3 pm on Sunday) and from 7 pm to 9 pm (9.30 pm on Friday and Saturday). Telephone: 01865 407847.

- **HOW TO GET THERE:** Clifton Hampden is on the A415 between Abingdon and Dorchester. The Barley Mow is just across the bridge on the right as the road bends.
- **PARKING:** There is a car park 50 yards to the south.
- **LENGTH OF THE WALK:** 2$^1/_2$ miles. Maps: OS Pathfinder 1136 Abingdon; OS Landranger 164 Oxford (inn GR 548954).

THE WALK

On approaching the bridge, having turned left out of the pub, it is best to face the oncoming traffic. On the far side go left through a gate and down onto the towpath. Do not go under the bridge but upstream along the towpath.

After a short distance the river divides into the Old Thames over to the left and the Clifton Cut ahead. The cut, which avoids the bends around the back of Long Wittenham, opened in 1822 following the success of a similar cut upstream at Culham which had carried the navigation channel for a decade. But the village is not forgotten for at Clifton Lock in summer there may be secondhand books on sale in aid of Long Wittenham's mainly 13th-century church.

But, well before entering the cut to pass through the lock, look back at the bridge with Clifton Hampden church seen above. Continue past the lock. There is a Conservancy gate before the way passes over the end of a bridge leading to the island created by the cut. On approaching the end of the channel, and just before drawing level with the Old Thames beyond the weir, turn sharp right down the bank

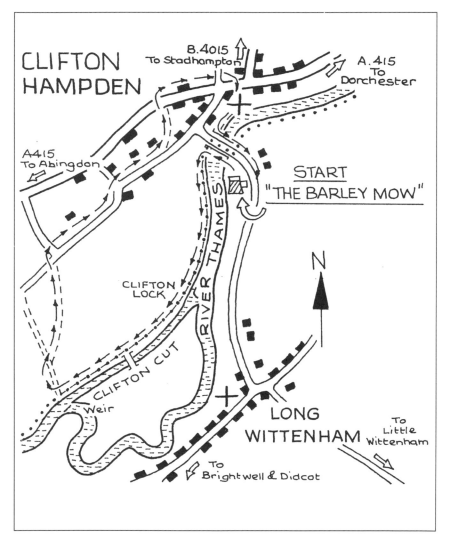

to head inland, leaving the Thames Path.

Keep forward by a fence through gateways to cross a field and go through a gap over a stream. Here the official footpath turns half right across the huge field although most walkers use the main track ahead which later turns right. To the west, behind you, is the spire of Appleford church below the looming Didcot Power Station. The main path and the line of the public footpath converge at a gateway just before a junction of farm roads. Keep forward on the rough track which enjoys a concrete surface as it passes a cottage and a barn. The farm road meets the village at a bend by the vineyard.

Keep ahead along the road and after 250 yards look for a path bearing off to the left to run up along the back of thatched cottages. Take this rising path which reveals some surprise tiling at the back of the cottages. The path turns sharply left to run alongside the grounds of Hampden House to the right.

At the main road go right past the Hampden House entrance and the village noticeboard by the bus stop. Across the road is the Plough, the village's other famous pub. The building is probably at least 17th century and is open all day, offering food at any time.

Go right at the junction to pass the post office. Just beyond, on the same side, are steps leading up to the church on high ground. There was a modest church here early in the 13th century but it was drastically remodelled by George Gilbert Scott in the 19th century. The Manor House just beyond the churchyard was intended by Scott to be the parsonage. The best view of the river and bridge is from the church.

Continue along the road which has a raised boarded walk for use during flooding. Cross the bridge to return to the Barley Mow.

THAMES PATH - CLIFTON HAMPDEN TO OXFORD (14 MILES)

From the bridge at Clifton Hampden the Thames Path is on the north bank, passing both Sutton Courteney and Abingdon. The lock and weir upstream of Abingdon provides the crossing just ahead of the old towpath crossing. From here the Path is on the south bank all the way north to Oxford.

OXFORD

The Head of the River

❦

The river Thames divides into numerous streams at Oxford which explains why, unlike other towns, today's river is on the outskirts of the city. Oxford was built on a river but that stream, which once surrounded the castle, is almost forgotten. The Osney Abbey channel has become the navigation route. Another stream is the Trill Mill Stream which runs underground before emerging behind the Head of the River pub. This walk follows the old and new Thames through the City starting at Folly Bridge where Lewis Carroll set out in 1862 on his upstream trip to Godstow during which the Alice tale emerged.

The Head of the River dates from at least the 1820s, when nearby Folly Bridge was built, but the house has only been a pub since 1977 when its name was decided after 2,700 suggestions had been sent to the *Oxford Mail.* The title is shared with the winning crew of the annual

Eights Week bumper races just downstream from here. Upstairs at the pub there is the twin scull which saw success in the 1908 Olympics. The local Headington stone building was once called Wharf House and in 1858 it became Salter Brothers' boatyard as the surviving crane outside among the tables reminds the visitor. The ground floor is surprisingly cosy with walls covered in old Thames photographs and advertising signs. Even the toilet corridor is packed with pictures which include a rare print of the 1810 rebuilding of Wallingford Bridge. In the bar area the floor is carpeted with large rugs.

There is an extensive menu with seven vegetarian dishes as well as lemon chicken and Hungarian goulash. The Oxford Blue ploughman's takes the form of a cottage loaf with butter, a generous wedge of blue cheese, a slice of tomato, pickle, lettuce and an apple. There is a children's menu and puddings include apple and sultana wholewheat crumble. The Head of the River, a Fuller's house, is open on Monday to Saturday from 11.30 am to 3 pm and 5.30 pm to 11 pm but all day, 11 am to 11 pm, in summer. Sunday times are always 12 noon to 3 pm and 7 pm to 10.30 pm. Food is available at lunchtime from 12 noon to 2.30 pm but in summer also in the evening until 9 pm. Telephone: 01865 721600.

- **HOW TO GET THERE:** Oxford is on the A40. The pub is next to Folly Bridge at the south end of St Aldate's. Oxford station is in Botley Road near Osney Bridge on the walk.
- **PARKING:** The city car parks are nearby.
- **LENGTH OF THE WALK:** 3 miles. Maps: Oxford Estate Publications Street Map; OS Pathfinder 1116 Oxford; OS Landranger 164 Oxford (inn GR 515066).

THE WALK

Cross Folly Bridge to go down the towpath, also the Thames Path, on the right which runs under a crane and past Jubilee Terrace. Pass under a footbridge which was built in 1886 to carry pipes between the gasworks which were on both banks. The next bridge is a former railway bridge for the gasworks sidings. Opposite, immediately upstream of this bridge, there is the mouth of a stream which may have been the main flow. The present navigation between here and Port Meadow, north of Oxford, was first dug by Osney Abbey around 1227 to drive its mill and enlarged in 1790.

Round another bend there is the main line railway bridge dating from 1850 and rebuilt in 1898. At the end of the footbridge spanning

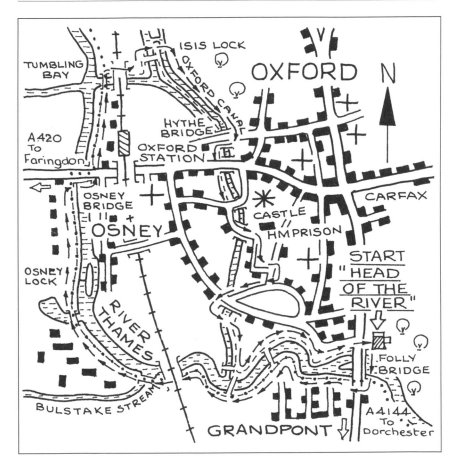

Bulstake Stream is a monument recalling a 21 year old man who died whilst saving two boys from drowning in 1889. Across the water is the start of the mill stream. The towpath occasionally has a horse trotting here with its mounted police officer.

Later the towpath crosses the weir stream to Osney Lock giving a view ahead of a derelict red brick mill and a 14th-century stone building with a high roof which is the remains of Osney Abbey. Beyond the lock the path is over the weirs and past the Waterman's Arms. Follow the line of riverside houses to reach Osney Bridge. Go up the steps over the braid to the road and cross the bridge.

At once go left to rejoin the towpath. The path, along backgardens with a view across to allotments, leads to a footbridge at Tumbling Bay – a male bathing spot until 1892 when both sexes were allowed.

Cross the narrow arched footbridge and leave the Thames Path by turning right to follow Sheepwash Channel. Go under the very low railway bridge and across an old level crossing, still flanked by gates. Beyond is a permanently open railway swing bridge complete with rails on rotting sleepers. The path bears round to the left to cross a footbridge. At once go right over Isis Lock which links the Oxford Canal to the Thames.

The path ahead is the Oxford Canal towpath which runs between the Thames' old channel to the right and the Oxford Canal to the left where there are always several houseboats. After 1/4 mile the path runs up to a road at Hythe Bridge which was a major loading point for Thames barges.

Turn right over the bridge and then left across the road to follow the Thames spur. Keep ahead across Park End Street and along Fisher Row. At a junction there is Quaking Bridge to the left – as a wooden bridge it used to shake – and in St Thomas' Street to the right Morrells brewery on the bank of the Wareham Stream – yet another Thames braid.

Continue ahead along Paradise Street where the water runs on the left beneath the castle which was once surrounded by a moat fed by the Thames. In 1142 Matilda escaped from the castle across frozen water, dressed in white to merge with the snowy landscape. The walk continues ahead over a bridge and right into Paradise Square. Walk to the far end and turn left to a junction with Norfolk Street. Turn right and soon bear right by a car park to go behind the Duke of York to cross the main road, Thames Street, just before the bridge – there is a green man crossing across the bridge to the right.

Go between the barriers to again follow the stream on the right which runs past houses and soon joins the main Thames. The path passes under the former railway bridge. Opposite is the towpath. At first the path is tree fringed. Later there are a couple of gates to go through before the path runs up behind the former Folly Bridge toll-house built in 1844. The Head of the River is opposite.

THAMES PATH - OXFORD TO BABLOCK HYTHE (9 MILES)

From Tumbling Bay, on this walk, the Thames Path remains on the same side for only a short distance before crossing to the south side on a footbridge just below Binsey. The Path stays by the river on the south side as far as Pinkhill Lock.

BABLOCK HYTHE

The Ferryman Inn

The Ferryman is an example of how a riverside pub and ferry can be successfully revived. This route makes use of the historic ferry and a stretch of towpath which is not part of the Thames Path to reach Pinkhill Lock. The return is over fields and along a bridleway used by the official Thames Path.

There has been a pub here at least since the days of an abbey at nearby Eynsham. Bablock Hythe is sometimes spelt as 'Bablock-hithe' or even as one word 'Bablockhythe' and the pub has changed its name several times. It was the Chequers for years before briefly becoming the Ferry Inn and now the Ferryman. The ferry, mentioned by Matthew Arnold in 1853 in *The Scholar Gypsy*, had been running continuously since about AD 950 when in 1965 it ceased after the craft sank. In these post-war years it carried three cars at a time and queues built up on Sunday afternoons. The service was resumed briefly in 1981 for foot passengers but for most of the Eighties the pub was closed. In 1992 the pub reopened under its present name and the ferry was again revived. There are historic pictures of the ferry in the main bar overlooking the river.

The pub has been rebuilt at least twice this century and its exterior is now like a modern private house so it's almost a surprise to find two bars inside. The furnishing is simple with crossed oars on the wall. In summer you can sit outside on the terrace. The menu includes soup which comes with warm bread, pâté and hot toast, jacket potatoes with tuna mayonnaise or cheese and beans and BLT baguettes served with salad and crisps. There is also a restaurant. This is a freehouse with Greene King and guest beers. The weekday opening hours are 11.30 am to 3.30 pm and 6.30 pm to 11 pm, all day in summer, from 11 am to 11 pm. The Sunday hours are always 12 noon to 3.30 pm and 6.30 pm to 10.30 pm. Food is available at lunchtime until 3 pm and from 6.30 pm to 10 pm. Telephone: 01865 880028.

- **HOW TO GET THERE:** Bablock Hythe is signposted off the B4449 just south of Stanton Harcourt in Oxfordshire. There is a limited bus service from Oxford. Bablock Hythe can be approached by ferry from the opposite bank by way of a bridleway from Cumnor which is served by buses from Oxford. Instructions for summoning the boat are on a tree.
- **PARKING:** There is a car park at the Ferryman Inn.
- **LENGTH OF THE WALK:** 5 miles. Maps: OS Pathfinder 1116 Oxford; OS Landranger 164 Oxford (inn GR 435043).

THE WALK

Ask the bar staff if you can be taken across the river on the ferry. (You should note that it does not run during adverse winter conditions when it can be difficult to hold the motorised craft against strong current and wind.)

Once on the far bank turn left to cross a stile and follow the towpath north. After 1½ miles the caravans on the far bank give way to countryside as the towpath runs level with the vast Farmoor Reservoir. Beyond a footbridge the river is briefly screened by trees before reaching the reservoir intake known as Skinner's Bridge after the family who ran a lonely thatched pub called the Fish on this bank. The footbridge was on the site of Skinner's Weir, or lock, which was removed in 1880.

The short cut ahead should be resisted in order to be faithful to the

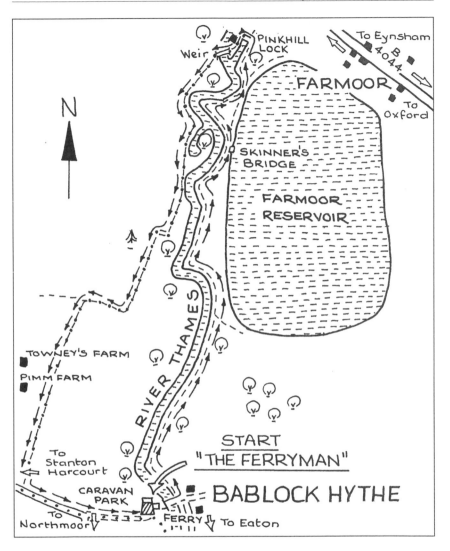

towpath and to see down an old lock cut passed later on the return route. Before a final right turn to approach the lock there is a view down a backwater which still carried through navigation a century ago. Soon after a stile there is Pinkhill Lock.

At the lock join the Thames Path by going left through a gate marked 'permitted path' and over the upstream lock gates. Go forward and bear half left onto grass to go past a lamppost and through the trees to cross the weir. On the far side there is a stile. Go half left

81

across a large field to meet the river again beyond another stile. Keep by the river to go over a couple of stiles ahead. The far bank was part of an island. Here bear half right and soon the path runs alongside the old channel noted earlier. The path joins the present navigation again at a point where the lost Skinner's Bridge crossed.

Look out for a lonely post which marks where the path veers away from the water – or rather keeps ahead as the river bends away. Walk to the far corner of the large field where there is a farm gate. Go through the gate and bear round to the right with the track to cross a stream. Now bear half left across to the far corner of this smaller field. In the corner there are two gates. Do not go through the wooden one – where in winter there may be a view of both the church tower and Pope's Tower at Stanton Harcourt – but through the waymarked gate to continue south.

Follow the hedge on the right which gives way to a gate and stile. Go over this stile on the right to follow a hedged road. Round the bend, at a junction, go through a narrow bridleway gate on the left. Continue south through six fields and a series of gates for almost a mile to reach a lane. Turn left and at a junction continue forward past a caravan site to reach the Ferryman Inn.

THAMES PATH - BABLOCK HYTHE TO NEWBRIDGE (4 MILES)

The Thames Path continues with the towpath on the same side as the Ferryman as far as Newbridge.

NEWBRIDGE
The Rose Revived

❧❦❧

*N*ewbridge is just a bridge with a pub at each end. The bridge with its six
pointed arches is not 'new', having been built in the mid 13th century, but
it's newer than upstream Radcot Bridge. From the upstream side there is a
view down onto the river Windrush on which stone from Taynton was
brought on barges for the bridge building. The walk crosses the medieval
bridge and takes the towpath upstream before turning south to climb a hill
and then return to the river over field paths. The route allows the much
photographed bridge to be seen from several angles.

The Rose Revived has been a pub since at least the Stuart period
although the building may date from the 14th century. It has been
called the Crown and the Fair House after annual Michaelmas fairs held
in the adjoining field. The present pub name when found elsewhere
usually refers to the restoration of the monarchy in 1660 but here a
publican named Rose is said to have reopened the pub. Another claim

is that the rival Maybush on the other end of the bridge had shorter hours so that local people tended to cross over for a reviving pint. However, a sign painted in 1919 by Alfred Parsons RA, and only recently replaced, showed roses being revived with Morland ale.

The interior has Victorian style wallpaper and some Thames pictures and maps. Outside there are weeping willows and a colourful garden. This is a very popular pub with both walkers and those afloat. The inn has accommodation and overnight moorings are nearby.

The food for those arriving at all hours and in all seasons includes soup with hot bread, ploughman's and filled baguettes. The main courses include at least three vegetarian dishes. A separate children's menu has Luscious Lasagne and Sea Stars both served with chips and baked beans or peas. Afternoon tea is also available. As the sign suggests, this is a Morland house with Morland Original, Old Speckled Hen and Old Masters from the Abingdon brewery. The Rose Revived is open all day from 11 am to 11 pm (Sunday 12 noon to 10.30 pm) with food served until 10 pm. Telephone: 01865 300221.

- **HOW TO GET THERE:** Newbridge is in Oxfordshire on the A415 between Standlake and Kingston Bagpuize. Buses from Oxford stop at the south end of Tuck's Lane in nearby Longworth.
- **PARKING:** There is a car park at the Rose Revived.
- **LENGTH OF THE WALK:** 3 miles. Maps: OS Pathfinder 1115 Witney (South) and Carterton and 1116 Oxford; OS Landranger 164 Oxford (inn GR 404014).

THE WALK

Cross the bridge to reach the Maybush which was originally the toll-house where a hermit collected tolls for the Benedictine monks from Paris who had built the crossing. The Maybush also has Morland ale and bar food.

Turn down the side of the inn and go over the Thames Conservancy footbridge and its gate. A causeway bears round towards the river. It is worth looking back occasionally to see the beautiful setting of the bridge. There is a kissing-gate and a Conservancy gate before the way runs below a slope and through trees to a bend in the river. You leave the Thames Path at a gated footbridge leading to a meadow.

At once go left to find a stile. A path runs over a footbridge and uphill into a field. Keep ahead along the side (right) of the field to cross a track at the far end. Continue forward on a now enclosed track which climbs up wooded Harrowdown Hill. The trees are to the right whilst to

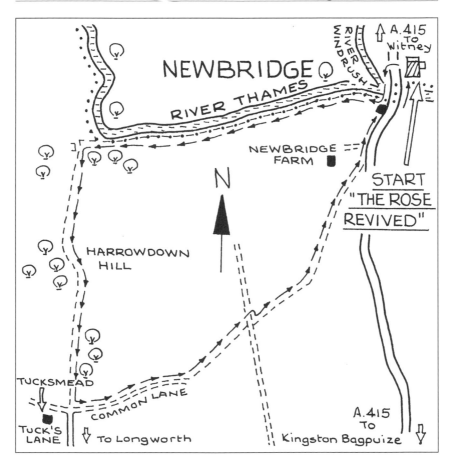

the left there is a panoramic view over the countryside. The path runs gently, with a double bend, downhill to a junction by the entrance to Tucksmead – the lonely house used to be Tuck's Mead.

Turn left to pass the end of Tuck's Lane (right) leading to Longworth village and keep forward on an also unmarked bridleway known as Common Lane. Still keep ahead when the way narrows. The path leads to a field. Follow the side (right) to a T-junction. Here go right through double gates and at once left through more double gates. Now the hedge is to the left. After a second gate bear left to keep by the side of the field. Another gate leads into a field where the distant traffic lights at Newbridge's narrow bridge can sometimes be seen through the trees. Head across this field to a gate at the opposite corner. Once through the gate join the road either by crossing the ditch or using the old footbridge to the right. Go left along the road (walking on the right side to face oncoming traffic) for a short distance to pass the entrance to Newbridge Farm and reach the flood bridge. Beyond the traffic lights is the Maybush. Cross the bridge for the Rose Revived.

🔔 THAMES PATH - NEWBRIDGE TO LECHLADE (15 MILES)

After crossing the river at Newbridge, the Thames Path stays on the south bank all the way to Duxford. A diversion takes the Path back to the Thames at Tenfoot Bridge where the towpath is at its loneliest on the north side to Tadpole. The next crossing is at Rushey Lock to allow the Path to continue on the south side to Radcot. From here the Path is on the north bank to pass Kelmscot before reaching St John's Bridge, within sight of Lechlade, where it crosses to the south bank again.

LECHLADE
The Trout

☙❦❧

*T*his is not a long walk because plenty of time is needed at the pub to enjoy
a meal and the surroundings. After passing the highest lock on the Thames,
guarded by Old Father Thames, there is one of the finest stretches of
towpath on the river. Beyond the former toll bridge the route takes you into
Lechlade with its interesting shops, including its fine village bakery, as well
as the landmark church. The return is along an ancient path over
meadows.

The Trout's building dates from about 1220 when it was part of St
John's Priory which stood on the north side of the Kelmscot road
behind the pub. The monastery had charge of the new stone Thames
bridge replacing a wooden crossing. Edward IV closed the community
of St John, leaving one person in charge of the bridge, and the living
accommodation later became Ye Sygne of St John the Baptist. In 1704
the pub, holding the monks' fishing rights, changed its name to the

Trout. By 1830 the landlord was also looking after, not the bridge, but the lock.

Outside there is an old walnut tree and in summer a marquee for extra space. The garden, divided by part of the fast moving weir stream, has water on three sides and boats for hire in season. Appropriately the bridge, rebuilt in 1886, provides the rising garden wall on the third side of the garden.

Inside, the low-beamed inn is panelled, and appropriately there are stuffed fish and fishing prints on the walls and live goldfish. The Trout has long been noted for its food, which is all individually prepared. The extensive menu chalked up over the fireplace includes home-made soups such as leek and Stilton, pâté, local trout and vegetarian dishes. A separate children's menu features Cap'n Bob's fish fingers and Old MacDonald's Farmhouse Lunch. The board can have as many as six puddings from rice pudding to double chocolate fudge cake. This is a Courage house with real ale and guest beers. The inn is open on weekdays from 10 am to 3 pm and 6 pm to 11 pm and the Sunday hours are 12 noon to 3 pm and 7 pm to 10.30 pm. Food is served until 10 pm. Telephone: 01367 52313.

- **HOW TO GET THERE:** The inn is by St John's Bridge on the A417 east of Lechlade in Gloucestershire.
- **PARKING:** The pub's car park is reached by way of the lane at the back, signposted 'Kelmscot'.
- **LENGTH OF THE WALK:** 2 miles. Maps: OS Landranger 163 Cheltenham and Cirencester; OS Pathfinder 1135 Faringdon (inn GR 224992).

THE WALK

Cross the road outside the pub to walk over St John's Bridge, facing the oncoming traffic. On the far side go right through a gate and down a stepped path to St John's Lock. This is the last and highest on the river with Old Father Thames, made for the 1851 Great Exhibition, at the side – he came here in 1974 after 16 lonely years at the source.

Go through the gate at the end of the lock compound and after a short distance cross a footbridge, once spanning a braid of the river Cole which enters higher up, to leave Oxfordshire and enter Wiltshire. As you follow the winding river, there is a view of the Lechlade church spire. Compton Mackenzie wrote 'the spire of the church remained so long in sight' in his novel *Guy and Pauline*. After a gate the towpath is

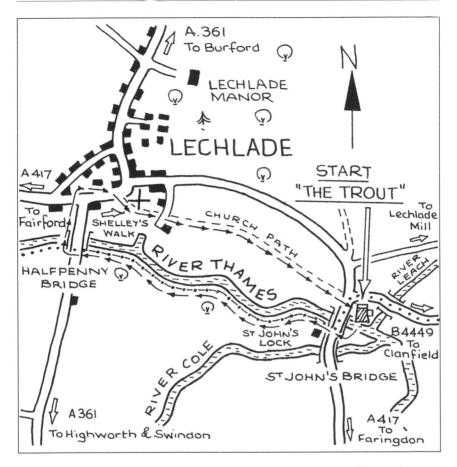

by fields. Opposite at one point is a lonely wartime pillbox. This is a good stretch to see swans and herons.

Before the bridge there is a clear view across the water to the archway of Lechlade's New Inn where the poet Shelley stayed in 1815, having rowed from Windsor. Go under Halfpenny Bridge to find steps leading up to the road. The crossing, known as Halfpenny Bridge because of the original toll levied at the toll-house, was built in 1793 just after the canal opened – hence the high arch.

Leaving the Thames Path here, cross the river to walk up to the T-junction at the High Street and turn right for the Market Square and the church.

Lechlade is still a village-size country town with good basic shops in Burford Street off the Market Square – an ironmonger's, a butcher selling home-made sausages and a fine baker's shop which also has local cheese. The church dates from 1476 and on the vestry door inside is the pomegranate symbol of Catherine of Aragon who held the manor. At the back of the church are the words of Shelley's poem *Stanzas in Lechlade Churchyard*, written at the New Inn.

Walk down Shelley's Walk at the side of the church. On the wall of Church Cottage, to the left, there is a plaque recalling Shelley's late night walk in the churchyard. Beyond the church is a view of a fine gazebo in the garden of the early 18th-century Church House which had a wharf behind for landing goods from London.

Shelley's Walk is the beginning of an almost straight path leading directly to the Trout. The full ¼ mile through fields is mainly metalled and known as Church Path or Bridge Walk – before Halfpenny Bridge was built there was only St John's Bridge. After the lane (leading to a school) and the kissing-gate there is in winter a view to the left to Lechlade Manor. Over a stile the river can be seen to the right. Beyond a second stile the path is straight and through a tunnel of trees – welcome cover in hot weather.

At the far end the path crosses a bridge and meets a road. To the left there is the Gloucester county sign. The Trout is to the right.

THAMES PATH - LECHLADE TO THE SOURCE (22 MILES)

After Halfpenny Bridge, on the pub walk, the Thames Path continues past Lechlade to Inglesham where the towpath ends. There is an unpleasant road diversion to Upper Inglesham where a long bridleway takes the path back to the Thames at Hannington Bridge. The waymarking becomes important as the route, although still on the south side, is away from the river bank, as far as Water Eaton. From there the Path is on the north side and then the south to enter Cricklade. The exit from this Wiltshire town is by way of North Meadow and the Cotswold Water Park to Waterhay Bridge. The Path is then alongside the infant Thames through Ashton Keynes into Gloucestershire, past Somerford Keynes, through Ewen and past Kemble, where water may have disappeared in summer, to the source under a tree in a field outside Kemble.

WALK 20
COATES
The Tunnel House
❧

The Tunnel House is the nearest pub to the Thames' source and so it is often approached, as at the end of this walk, from the disused canal's towpath. This splendid circular route, full of interest, visits the official source after passing through the attractive Cotswold village of Coates.

The Tunnel House was built in local stone about 1780 at the instigation of the Earl of Bathurst for workmen who were to spend five years digging the two mile Thames and Severn Canal tunnel. The canal took navigation on beyond the shallow riverbed at Inglesham and past the Thames' source to join the Stroudwater Navigation. Salt from Droitwich and fruit from Evesham came through the tunnel to the Thames. This traffic was eventually reduced by the arrival of the railways and the last through boat passed in the tunnel in 1911. Today the Stroudwater and Severn Canal Trust, engaged on a long restoration programme, offer boat trips into the tunnel when the water level is high.

The pub's first customers were miners from Derbyshire and Cornwall, working day and night by candlelight. Now this is a local for Cirencester College agricultural students, farm workers – and walkers who have just completed the 180 mile Thames Path from London. This pub was a favourite of John Betjeman whose daughter Candida confesses that 'the romance of the place has never diminished for me'. The interior is a delightful jumble of furniture, Thames memorabilia, pictures and old advertising signs. There are also books, including the Bible, and old copies of *Hello!* and *Harpers*. In winter there are log fires.

The changing food menu might include fresh salmon fishcakes, steak and kidney pudding and 'probably the best chilli in the world', according to the landlord. There are always rolls – the sausage version is three sausages with salad. This is a freehouse with Archers Best, Smiles and Theakston Best among the many real ales. The Tunnel House is open on weekdays all day from 10 am to 11 pm except on Mondays and Tuesdays when there is a closure from 3 pm to 6.30 pm. Sunday hours are 12 noon to 10.30 pm. Food is usually served until 10 pm. Children are welcome. Telephone: 01285 770280.

- **HOW TO GET THERE:** The inn is at the end of a rough track off Tarlton Road at Coates, which is signposted off the A433 between Tetbury and Cirencester in Gloucestershire. The nearest station is Kemble, 2 miles away on the infant Thames. The walk can be joined by taking the Thames Path out of Kemble to the source.
- **PARKING:** There is a car park at the Tunnel House.
- **LENGTH OF THE WALK:** 3½ miles. Maps: OS Pathfinder 1133 Tetbury and 1113 Stroud; OS Landranger 163 Cheltenham (inn GR 967006).

THE WALK

Turn left out of the pub and cross the top of the tunnel. Just as the track has turned the corner go left through a gate (or over the stile) and up a bank to a stile at the top of the railway embankment. Walk down the ramp and, after listening for a train, cross the tracks and walk up to the stile on the far side. There is now the first glimpse of Coates church tower ahead behind a tree. The spire seen to the far right is Kemble church.

Walk ahead over the field to a gap in the stone wall ahead. Bear half right across the corner of the next field to follow a stone wall on the right. The path bears right to open out and reach the little Norman

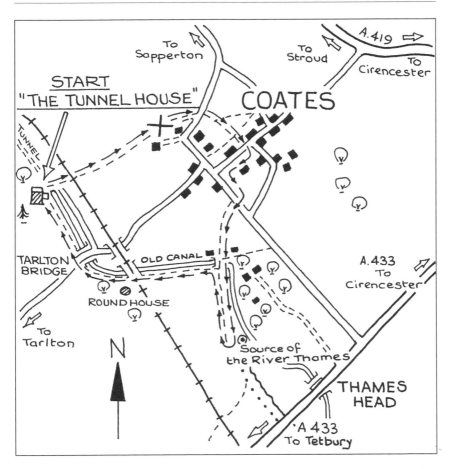

church which was here when the de Coates family gave its name to the village. The tower was added in the Tudor period.

Continue past the church and along the concrete farm road to meet Tarlton Road. Cross over and go through the kissing-gate. Stay ahead on the right side of the field to pass through another kissing-gate. The trees over to the left are in the Earl of Bathhurst's Cirencester Park. At a third kissing-gate go ahead over a field to a gate leading to a short path running between houses in Coates main street. To the left is the former school with its clock and the war memorial. Go right to pass the now redundant Edward VII postbox in the wall and the village hall.

At a T-junction go left and after 300 yards (beyond the Beech Cottage entrance to the left) go right over a stone stile by a gate. Follow the stone wall on the right as the path gently drops downhill. At the bottom of the field go over a stile in the wall. Here there is a view over the start of the Thames valley and the trees lining the canal. At once go left to follow the wall on the left which runs downhill to a stile by a gate at farm buildings. Keep forward on a track to cross the disused canal.

The return route to the pub is to the right on the far side of the bridge but to see the Thames' source $1/4$ mile away keep ahead on the track to reach a field. Stay by the field boundary to the left and go over the two ladderstiles by the track gates. After a stile by a third gate go slightly left to find the (probably dry) source of the river Thames under an ash tree below the bank of the old canal on the left. There is a Thames Water stone which replaced Old Father Thames now found at St John's Lock (see Walk 19). In dry periods water can usually be seen ahead about a mile downstream. Retrace the route to the old canal bridge and go left to find the very wooded towpath.

Soon after passing under the Kemble-Gloucester railway line there is a former gate stop and round house dating from 1789. The canal company abandoned these unusual tied cottages when staff objected to the round rooms. The ground soon rises and beyond Tarlton Bridge, which carries the road to the pub, there is a deep cut leading to the Sapperton Tunnel and the Tunnel House inn.

Tourist Information Centres

Richmond – Old Town Hall, Whittaker Avenue, Richmond, Surrey TW9 1TP. Tel: (0181) 940 9125.

Kingston-upon-Thames – Market House, Market Place, Kingston-upon-Thames, Surrey KT1 1JS. Tel: (0181) 547 5592.

Staines – General Administration Office, Borough of Spelthorne, Knowle Green, Staines, Middlesex TW18 1XB. Tel: (01784) 451499.

Windsor – 24 High Street, Windsor, Berks SL4 1LH. Tel: (01753) 852010.

Marlow – Court Garden Leisure Complex, Pound Lane, Marlow, Bucks SL7 2AE. Tel: (01628) 483597.

Henley-on-Thames – Town Hall, Market Place, Henley-on-Thames, Oxon RG9 2AQ. Tel: (01491) 578034.

Reading – Town Hall, Blagrave Street, Reading, Berks RG1 1QH. Tel: (01734) 566266.

Wallingford – Town Hall, Market Place, Wallingford, Oxon OX10 0EG. Tel: (01491) 826972.

Abingdon – 25 Bridge Street, Abingdon, Oxon OX14 3HN. Tel: (01235) 522711.

Oxford – The Old School, Gloucester Green, Oxford, Oxon OX1 2DA. Tel: (01865) 726871.

Cirencester – Corn Hall, Market Place, Cirencester, Gloucestershire GL7 2NW. Tel: (01285) 654180.

Accommodation

Plenty of bed and breakfast is available near the Thames. Several of the featured pubs offer accommodation and Tourist Information Centres can provide full local lists. Below is a select list:

Windsor – The Laurells, 22 Dedworth Road, SL4 5AH. Tel: (01753) 855821.

Marlow – 5 Pound Lane, SL7 2AF. Tel: (01628) 482649.

Aston – The Flower Pot, Aston, Henley-on-Thames, RG9 3DG. Tel: (01491) 574721.

Henley – The Jolly Waterman, Reading Road, RG9 1EL. Tel: (01491) 573055.

Reading – Crescent Hotel, 35 Coley Avenue (on Path between bridges) RG1 6LL. Tel: (01734) 507980.

Wallingford – The George, High Street, Wallingford, Oxon OX10 0BS. Tel: (01491) 836665.

Dorchester – The George, High Street, Dorchester-on-Thames, Oxon OX10 7HH. Tel: (01865) 340404.

Clifton Hampden – The Barley Mow, Clifton Hampden, Abingdon, Oxon OX14 3EH. Tel: (01865) 407847.

Bablock Hythe – The Ferryman Inn, Northmoor, Oxon OX8 1BL. Tel: (01865) 880028.

Newbridge – The Rose Revived, Newbridge, Whitney, Oxon OX8 6QD. Tel: (01865) 300221.

Lechlade – The New Inn, Market Square, Lechlade, Gloucestershire GL7 3AB. Tel: (01367) 252296.

YHA

Rotherhithe – (opposite the Spice Island): Island Yard, Salter Road, London SE16 1LY. Tel: (0171) 232 2114.

Windsor – Edgeworth House, Mill Lane, Clewer, Windsor SL4 5JH. Tel: (01753) 861710.

Streatley – (near Goring): Hill House, Reading Road, Streatley, Reading RG8 9JJ. Tel: (01491) 872278.